SPIRITUAL
UNFOLDMENT
I

· Some further books of White Eagle's teaching

SPIRITUAL UNFOLDMENT

I

How to Discover the Invisible Worlds
and Find the Source of Healing

WHITE EAGLE

THE WHITE EAGLE PUBLISHING TRUST
LISS · HAMPSHIRE · ENGLAND

Original Edition published in June 1942
reprinted 1944, 1946
Second edition, revised, with new matter,
first published in November 1961;
Eighth impression 1986

© *Copyright, White Eagle Publishing Trust 1961*
ISBN 0 85487 012 1

Printed in Great Britain
at the University Printing House, Oxford

CONTENTS

∽

INTRODUCTION
(1961)

The greater part of my life has been devoted, through study and practice, to the technique of penetrating the veil which lies between man's existence on the physical plane and another, more perfect life in the unseen spiritual spheres immediately surrounding the earth. It is generally thought that only after death is man allowed to know anything of these higher and finer worlds which surround us; and that when he has passed onward, he is debarred from communicating with his friends on earth.

In this book White Eagle shows us the way towards experiencing for ourselves while still on earth the beauties of this more perfect life; and how an etheric bridge may be built between men incarnate and discarnate to their mutual joy and well-being.

He teaches that true clairvoyance is a deep spiritual experience. While it is admitted that there is a certain type of spontaneous psychic 'seeing' which appears to function in animals as well as in man, a vast difference lies between this spontaneous 'seeing,' and true spiritual vision or clairvoyance. The former can be illusory, the latter is the result of knowledge and training of the spiritual faculties latent within every soul. By following White Eagle's guidance we learn that there are numerous levels of vision-awareness or consciousness of another state of life. This awareness can range from the mere impression of some passing influence or shadowy form, lights or clouds of colour, to the clear vision of bright pulsating forms of highly evolved beings, and of beautiful landscapes, temples of worship, music and art schools and colleges, which are part of the normal environment of a community in this higher life, beyond death.

Beyond again lie higher mental planes and celestial realms impossible to describe in earthly language. To be able to see these glories, and to retain a memory clear enought to leave an impression on the physical brain afterwards, requires both steady persistent effort in the practice of the technique of spiritual unfoldment, and constant pursuit of the spiritual life. It is made plain in these messages that by 'spiritual life' is meant God-aspiring life, wholesome, clean-living, disciplined and well-balanced. Truly the man of earth in search of spiritual illumination must manifest God to the best of his ability; he must worship God with all his heart and soul and mind, and by love of God and his neighbour promote a spirit of goodwill and kindliness in the community generally. White Eagle endeavours to show us that the development of power to penetrate reliably the dark veils which lie between the physical state of life and the spirit worlds, depends not only upon the acquisition of knowledge, but also upon the degree of simple Christ-liness developed within the soul.

Devotion to the spiritual life and constancy of endeavour to master the technique of 'going within' to find the heart of truth, to find eternal life, brings its due reward; man finds himself endowed with gifts of the spirit which make him free to contact the inner spiritual world at will, and convince him, beyond all shadow of doubt, of the immortality of the soul.

During nearly half a century I have been helped to develop spiritual gifts which have enabled me to bridge the gulf between the two states of life, and to bring back knowledge of the higher worlds. White Eagle, who is my spirit Guide and Teacher, has for over thirty years communicated to me, and through me, knowledge of how these higher faculties of man may be safely developed and used for the benefit of mankind; and to add to the happiness and harmony of mortal life.

Of these communications a few were selected and published during the last war in four volumes under the title of *Spiritual Unfoldment*, a series which proved so popular that several printings were exhausted. The books have now been out of print for a number of years, during which time many requests have come for their republication. Not the least among these requests is one from White Eagle himself, who has expressed an earnest hope that his message from the spirit spheres of life should be made available to all who are searching for knowledge and understanding how to contact the life of the unseen worlds, and gain comfort and help from this contact.

This newly-produced volume of *Spiritual Unfoldment* contains most of the matter from Books One and Two of the original edition, revised and re-arranged, but omitting the section on the nature kingdom which it is planned to incorporate in a later book. It also contains much that is new, notably the chapters on Healing and upon the Human Aura. The bulk of the messages here presented were given through me by White Eagle in the early days of our combined work, in the form of lectures to students; but the new matter, some of which has never before been published in any form, is taken from his more recent teachings.

In White Eagle's name I offer you this book, in the hope that you will find in its pages much that will console and inspire you. I write in all sincerity, and with kind wishes.

GRACE COOKE

I

A SIMPLE APPROACH

As we commune with spirit we open our hearts to love. We know that love is the way to spiritual unfoldment; and therefore we pray to God, our Father and Mother, that we may become love; and in becoming more loving we shall become wiser, and so stronger in the power of God. May this Holy Trinity of love, wisdom and power become manifest in our hearts and lives. Amen.

The fundamental purpose of man's life is that he may find truth, truth which will be unveiled to him by his own inner-self. As we search for this truth which lies buried deep within, the barriers erected by the outer-self will vanish and we shall become free, free to hold communion with those we love in the beyond; free to contact the cosmic rays of life-force and healing; free to use them in the service of our brother man; free to become *en rapport* with those beings who minister to humanity from the spirit.

   The pathway which climbs the mountain side to the heavenly summit is long and steep;

and until man obtains a glimpse of the glory which awaits him he is in travail on the planes of materialism. He suffers pain, sickness, isolation, limitation; he remains heir to fear, resentment, anxiety, and is afflicted by conflicts and wars. But no man need wait until after he is freed from the flesh to realise happiness and his true being. Indeed, unless man learns to seek the spirit while still on earth he will not find complete freedom or joy merely by discarding the physical body.

A glorious future awaits each soul, but it entails hard work—although even hard work can be very interesting. For instance, if you love music and long to express yourself through music, it becomes a joy to practise, to acquire mastery over your instrument. If you are wholly interested in something worthwhile you do not mind taking pains, nor do you count the cost of attainment. So it should be with this work spent upon your soul.

To work upon the soul does not always demand the setting apart of long periods for meditation. The way of meditation is not necessarily your way; but having decided upon your particular path, follow it steadfastly. Do not follow 'squirrel-tracks'; do not run hither and thither thinking that someone else has found a better path than yours and that you will try his. As children when plucking flowers flit from patch to patch in case some other child has found better flowers than they, so do children of earth rush hither and thither after the truths of the spirit.

This is not the way. For a time will come when your innermost voice will speak to you, saying: 'This is *my* path; here I shall find peace. I will pursue this path, come what may.' Having made your decision, you must abide by it. You will not always find this easy; but if you persist and are patient, and above all never lose faith, your path will lead you unerringly to your goal.

In following the spiritual path, you will have to learn to discriminate between the promptings of the worldly mind and the higher, God-mind, to distinguish the real from that which is unreal and transient. The worldly mind dwells within us all and causes us to doubt the reality of spiritual truth. Again and again as you progress in spiritual unfoldment, you will surely find that doubt will challenge you—doubt, posing as common sense, as scrupulous honesty which prefers plain truth to delusion. This doubting worldly mind will try to argue with you, suggesting that anything which your spiritual vision reveals to you cannot be proved and is only a figment of the imagination.

This mind of the body has its place and can be a sound enough guide within its limitations, once it has learnt to defer to the God-mind. Truth which the worldly mind would term 'pure nonsense' may be accepted and treasured by the spiritual mind. To the higher sense of the soul—man's intelligence as distinct from his intellect—it may appear as a rare gem of truth. So we must learn discrimination, and having rendered unto Caesar the worldly things which truly belong to Caesar, seek to find the pearl of truth.

Those who know and Those who do not know

A wise teacher has said that there are only two kinds of people in the world: *those who know and those who do not know*; those who are aware of God's presence everywhere, at all times, as a continual comfort and inspiration; who know that they can obtain guidance and enlightenment from higher worlds of wisdom and beauty: and those who, knowing nothing about these things, ignore or scoff at them, and live accordingly as if imprisoned in a dark room. Those of you who know, or at least are beginning to know, have earned your spiritual awareness through patient effort, experience and suffering.

Yet you must still be watchful and work to retain that knowledge, for while there is an urge which causes the light of the spirit to grow, there is also this mind of earth, which will urge you to doubt, condemn and even destroy the growing light in your heart. Man has to struggle hard and long until the light within becomes so powerful and strong that doubts can never again assail him.

The doubts and questionings which assail you are like the voice of the serpent in the Garden of Eden, which tempted Adam and Eve to eat of the fruits of earthliness and ignore their God.

Are we not all striving to 'listen in' to the voice of the spirit, even while we are continually assailed by the clamour of the outer world? Do not be put off by people who tell you there is no such thing as the spirit world, no such possibility as the healing of the sick by spiritual means. They who speak thus are dwellers in the darkness and do not know. As it is said in the Bible, 'The dead know not anything.' Send them the light of love and realise that later on they too will learn. Do not force your own opinions on them, because arguments seldom lead anywhere or convince anyone. These people mean well, but on the path *you* have chosen, you must remain loyal to the voice of the spirit.

What is your Motive?

Spiritual unfoldment should never be sought for purely selfish motives, or for love of sensation or from curiosity, but only because we realise that it can make us healthy in body and radiant in spirit, and therefore better equipped to help our fellow creatures. The underlying purpose behind spiritual training of any kind should be selfless and altruistic. Patience will be required, and also the realisation that you may never be called upon to do your work before the public, to impress others or win recognition or reward. Indeed, most of you will labour quietly behind the scenes; even a life tied to domesticity can be truly creative. Be very sure that all are placed in the exact position in earth life where they are most needed and where they will have opportunities for doing the most good. The unknown man or woman may contribute more to the advancement of the human race than one whose name is in everyone's mouth. The whole purpose of spiritual unfoldment is for the individual man so to train himself that he becomes a more powerful centre from which the love of God can radiate. Then he no longer hankers after the wonderful things that the 'I' can do. Instead he desires only that through him a greater love may be breathed forth into life.

A healthy Mind in a healthy Body

A point we would emphasise in spiritual unfoldment and in the preparation of the healer, is the
need for a healthy mind together with a healthy
body for those who would be channels for the
light. Any practice which depletes the body,
which causes the mind to run along unhealthy
channels, must be put aside. Correct spiritual
development will help to create health, and in
its turn a healthy mind will help in the unfoldment of the spiritual qualities and faculties.

Remember that we are all both receiving
and broadcasting stations; and while we are able
to respond to influences and impressions from
the invisible planes of life, we also react to worldly
influences and to the vibrations set in motion by
the thoughts and lives of others. We often allow
ourselves to become overshadowed or obsessed
by fear, anger, hatred and all manner of passions,
as well as by bodily ills. We do not always understand why we feel as we do, and although we try
hard we cannot overthrow our unknown adver-
sary. Truly we are then in an unhealthy state.

Are we speaking too directly? But you are
seeking spiritual development; you desire to

unfold your spiritual gifts, so you have to learn to use your instrument. As we have said, before you can play any musical instrument you have to master the technique; you must learn the art of words if you would use your pen, and master form and colour if you would paint pictures. So also must you be prepared to pay the price of spiritual development and undergo the training which spiritual development will demand of you. This entails a continual cleansing of your mental outlook until it manifests a degree at least of health and wholeness, or holiness. My dear ones, how can you expect to have a healthy body if your mind is unhealthy? You will reply that you know plenty of perfectly healthy people whose minds seem far from healthy. But this is only a question of time; health will not long endure if the mind lacks ease and harmony.

Therefore, always think healthily, constructively, optimistically. We do not mean with a foolish optimism, but happily and confidently, knowing that behind all the apparent confusion of earth life a divine purpose is at work, evolving the spiritual qualities in men. If your mind were trained more healthfully it would never be drawn down into a vortex of depression and fear: you would be positive in your thought, knowing that all works together for good, and that whatever comes along, good is always behind it.

Often you are upset and disturbed because so many things are awaiting your attention, and you work too hard *in your mind*. You do a piece of work a hundred times mentally when you need actually do it only once. You say to yourself again and again: 'I must do so and so,' but 'so and so' does not get done. Train yourself, then, to meet the work of the moment *when it comes*, and quietly do it. Do you see the importance of this quiet acceptance of what comes along, and doing it at the moment and finishing with it? It is better to put any task or problem right out of your mind until the opportunity comes to deal with it; but do get out of the habit of worrying, worrying, worrying over little pinpricks. In the majority of people the mind is like an untidy ragbag. It is not easy to receive impressions from the higher world into this conglomeration of odds and ends. If the brain is stuffed tight the rays of spiritual light which might penetrate are rebuffed. They may persist until at last in some quiet moment penetration is effected. But if the mind be crammed how can the man receive impressions from the higher worlds, or become aware of the angel at his side? Be in command, be the master. That is what we are all working for—mastership.

A Master is never disturbed or in a hurry. We find no disorder in his surroundings. Having become *master of himself* he naturally has control over the world about him, and so never suffers ill-health, never has a headache, or a cold or any ailment of that nature. You will say that we should not expect any one of you to reach this standard. No, dear ones, none of you are Masters, but this is the ideal towards which you strive.

Long ago, when men entered monasteries to devote their lives to God it was thought a sin to fall ill. In another life we can well remember brother Red Indian chieftains knew no sickness and did not leave their earthly bodies because of disease, but only when their particular incarnation had drawn to a close, and the time had come for a period of passivity and absorption in the life beyond. Then the spirit would withdraw from the body into a higher world for refreshment after labour. As the Ancient Mystery teaching says, 'We go from earth labour to refreshment in the heavens, and after refreshment we return again to labour on earth.'

Look forward to a time when you will become whole and healthy; it is your Father's wish that this should be so, and there is no reason why this cannot be attained during your present life.

When people come to us for guidance we may not always explain the principles which govern man's health and well-being. We therefore try to indicate a line of thought to which we feel that particular souls will respond most readily. We do not think it wise to hurl truths at our brother, so that he takes a long time to recover from the shock, so we usually speak gently, giving him the food of the spirit which we think he can digest *at that time*. Afterwards we watch. If the pupil proves earnest and strives to follow simple rules, little by little more is unfolded. There are gentle ways of helping others, and the truth which suits one is not suitable for all. There are however certain basic rules for physical well-being and spiritual training, which we will give you.

One rule concerns what you should eat. You know that man possesses subtler bodies in addition to his physical body, and his food supplies nourishment to the different types of atom composing the physical and etheric bodies. If he eats the coarser foods he stimulates the coarser atoms. Whereas, if his tastes incline him to eat only sun-nourished foods such as fruit, ripened corn, nuts and vegetables he will feed and nourish the higher aspects of his being and thus assist his spiritual unfoldment. The eating of coarser foods will make his training harder and longer—that is all.

From birth onwards to middle age and death the body is becoming congested with poisonous accumulations.

The foodstuffs that civilisation has produced, when assimilated into your body, tend to produce this clogged condition. The water you drink also has this effect. Foods of the wrong type tend to thicken the bloodstream and cause, in middle life and old age, much sluggishness. Your object, if you are on the spiritual path, is to purify the physical atoms; and if you want pure vehicles you must eat pure food.

It is better not to eat flesh because so often animals are killed under conditions of fear, and the blood, the red meat, will transmit to you the fears and the coarse vibrations. You would be very horrified if it were suggested to you that you should eat your brother at your side. You would think it a shocking thing, wouldn't you? There was a time when degenerate races did this, but you regard it as a depraved taste. In a little while the eating of the flesh of any living creature will be considered depraved taste, quite apart from the cruelty inflicted. Cruelty is a very important subject, and the one on the spiritual path steers clear of cruelty in *any* form. There

exists so much more cruelty than cruelty to our animal brethren. We are sorry to say that mankind does not realise the extent of the cruelties which it inflicts, not only upon animals, but upon its own kind.

We come now to the vexed question of smoking. We never say, 'Do this or that,' we only tell you what we know. Your choice depends upon yourself. Really it is better not to smoke, better for your whole being. For one thing, it contributes towards self-mastery if you can overcome the habit. Smoking tends to clog both the physical and the etheric bodies, and while we admit that there are those on the path who smoke and still make progress, they can function only on a limited plane. Smoking is a poison: but so also are tea and coffee. If you must have tea, have the variety called China or herb or maté tea. Nevertheless, we do not like fanaticism. We always advise the middle way, discrimination, balance, wisdom. But in all probability, after your feet have been set on the spiritual path, the more you know, the less you will be governed by the appetites of the flesh.

At the same time it is not the choice of food that matters most, but the nature of your thoughts and your general outlook on life. Remember that all your bodies, physical, mental,

astral and spiritual are the temple of the Holy
Spirit, of the God-within. Therefore you must
continually try to attune yourselves so that you
live on the God vibration, aspiring always to God.

Poise

The correct poise and stance of your physical
body can help you. For instance, if you train
yourself to stand straight, as all true Masons
should stand, with feet together at the correct
angle, with the weight resting on the balls of the
feet instead of on the heels, the spine naturally
straightens and becomes erect, bringing about
polarisation of all the bodies. If, when sitting,
you slump in your chair with your spine curled
up, although it may feel more comfortable (to
us it would be an impossible position), the spine
becomes weakened and the vertebrae so loose as
a result of this slovenly way of sitting, that however often spinal troubles are corrected they are
likely to recur.

By constant endeavour it can and will become habitual to stand and walk on the balls of
the feet, straight and erect, easily and happily. To
do this gives poise to the body and grace and
swing to the gait. Have you ever watched a Red
Indian walk? From this you could learn very

much about poise and movement.

You will also find it more comfortable in the long run to learn to sit straight, depending on your spine and not on the back of the chair for support. You have tried this, you say, and find it makes your back ache? This is because your back has weakened through not being properly used, but God has given you power in your spine to support your back comfortably and easily. Try for yourself and see what a difference it makes to your mental outlook when you hold yourself erect. The position seems to fill you with light, which is exactly what happens, because then the spiritual light can enter at the crown of the head and pass without hindrance through your spine to its base. Your feet, free and supple as they should be, are able to draw magnetism from the earth itself; for the feet are two important psychic centres, as are the hands. This magnetism circulating through your aura can help to give you the strength and vitality for which you long.

Whenever you are sitting for spiritual unfoldment the head should be erect, the spine straight, the hands loosely clasped, the body relaxed, the mind at peace. This will create a positive attitude which will protect you against negative forces.

Breathing

Many people die before their natural time because their bodies are filled with poison, due to
eating the wrong food, or caused by breathing
impure air over long periods and failing to exhale
it properly.

Yoga training has often been repudiated;
the Western body, it is said, needs its own particular form of development, and the Eastern method
is unsuitable to the West. But we would give you
help which will suit your Western body. It is not
an Eastern yoga, but one which will be found
sound and suitable for the pupil of the West.

Some people will advise you to avoid all
breathing exercises, but if you will follow our
plan only good will result. But you must do
exactly as we say and not make experiments on
your own account. It is not good during the
early stages to attempt to breathe too deeply or
to hold the breath too long, causing the heart to
palpitate and the head to become dizzy. It is not
good to cause a feeling of strain in your body.
Any exercise in breathing should be harmonious,
producing, not discomfort, but a sense of peace
and well-being. In spiritual training always seek
for harmony, always keep your elbows (meta-
phorically speaking) well tucked in, physically,

mentally and spiritually.

Few if any people *breathe out* and empty their lungs sufficiently. Far too many breathe only with the top of their lungs, retaining in the lower parts of the lungs an accumulation of stale and poisonous air. This is a bad habit which may continue for a whole lifetime. Learn to breathe deeply, and to exhale fully, but this will not become a habit without considerable application. You must also learn to breathe slowly, quietly, harmoniously, gradually drawing in the breath deeper and deeper until you fill and empty the lower part of the lungs, expanding the ribs fully as you inhale.

Here is an exercise for you: having first cleaned the nostrils, stand if possible before an open window. As you inhale each breath aspire to God, feel that God is entering into you. Then, as you exhale, send out your blessing upon all life. This in-breathing will cause the spiritual sunlight to fill and illumine you, and register on a chakra or psychic centre situated at the brow. From that centre you can mentally direct the light to the heart-centre in order to bring spiritual sunlight to the seed atom—of which we shall speak later—which rests in the human heart. Do this each day if you can, and for as long as you like, *but without strain*. As you train yourself to stand, sit and walk correctly and erectly you are also emphasising the correct spiritual posture—eyes shining, looking right into the light of the sun, so that you can see nothing else but the glory of the sun, the glory of the Christ. You see, not the confusion of the earthly minds around you, but only the blazing light of Christ. With spine erect and posture correct, breathe in this light upon which you are gazing—breathe it in and absorb it; then send it forth quite naturally to the suffering ones of earth.

You see, it is such a gentle and natural and peaceful process, when you become in tune and in harmony with it.

One last word: we have often told you to use plenty of water both inside and out. Oh! that we had the power to provide you all with a stream of crystal-clear, sun-impregnated water which you could drink and bathe in daily! Of course this is not possible when most of you live in crowded cities; but we well remember how much we all delighted in the crystal-clear streams in our own lands of long ago. A cold bath is a somewhat harsh alternative, and we would again advise you never to embark on anything which shocks the system unduly. Always work for harmony and do not fly to extremes. Very hot baths are also injurious; we suggest, therefore, that you reduce the temperature of your baths and have a brisk rub down afterwards. Enjoy it all, but not to the extent of tiring yourself.

Boiled or filtered water should be chosen for drinking purposes if possible, because city water is often charged with impurities and minerals injurious to bodily health, leaving harmful deposits behind them. Before your breathing exercises each morning sip a little water, and as you drink let there be a meaning in what you do. Think, '*I drink this sip of water: with this I am assimilating into my being the Divine Wisdom.*' Take another sip and think, '*I assimilate Divine Love!*' Take another and think, '*I am assimilating Divine Power!*' Thus with every sip you drink you can draw upon one aspect of the Godhead, and by so doing you will be continually cleansing your physical and subtler bodies. Then utter this prayer:

'*Breathe on me, Breath of God . . . that I in turn may live to bless all men, all living creatures, all life . . .*'

Then breathe in this Breath of God!

II

THE HUMAN AURA

We would speak now of the human aura, re-membering that it is only through the medium of the aura that those in spirit are able to com-municate with you.

Many different terms are used for the various subtler bodies of man, and the terms we use may be different from those you are used to in other schools of thought, but we will try to make the subject as simple as possible.

Unless you have a comprehensive know-ledge you are apt to misread the aura. For instance, the clairvoyant whose vision is just opening may see only an aura of a few inches, and of a bluish colour, emanating from the physical body, and declare that he is seeing the whole aura. What he sees is the vital life-force interpenetrating the physical body, which is used as a medium between the spiritual and the earth life. This particular aura, the etheric or vital body, is closely connected with the nervous system, and collects most of what later manifests as ill health of the physical body, holding fast to poisons put forth by the lower mind of man by wrong thinking, wrong eating, and wrong living.

Attached to the physical body is a certain form recognisable as the body-elemental. This is not an evil thing; it has its place in the evolution, not only of man but also of the lower forms of life. We have been asked how it is that when man is in a physical body the pull of evil seems so much stronger than the attraction, the aspiration to good. You will find the answer in this body- or desire-elemental, which is very strong in most men. Man has to learn in the course of his evolution that the higher self (which is only partially in evidence in most of us) must gain complete domination over the body-elemental. The home of the human ego is in the celestial body, the highest and purest aura of man. The bidding of the ego descends to man's consciousness as his intuition: you call it conscience. But the body-elemental is also assisting man in his evolution, as a kind of ballast which keeps him tied to earth. You all feel this pull, but it is not to be regarded as evil, for it forces growth of the spiritual or God-consciousness which we all come back on earth to unfold.

We have already spoken of the vital body, which is not really an aura but an emanation of the physical. This departs with the death of the physical body except for a small part which is drawn up into the highest aura, which we will call the celestial aura. The reason for this is that through its contact with earth it has absorbed certain lessons, which are retained to be used in future states of life, not necessarily in the heaven world, but in future incarnations.

The next body is the astral. The astral body is that usually seen by clairvoyants, who will describe the aura and say it has certain colours. Beyond the astral body or aura is the mental body, and beyond the mental aura the celestial body, called in some schools the 'causal' body.

The aura of the astral body is composed either of coarse or more refined matter, depending upon the quality of the human consciousness. If the body-elemental is very strong, holding great power, the astral aura will be coarse, and consequently the colours will be coarse rather than beautiful. When the soul can recognise the reality of the spiritual life and the purpose of its incarnation, then this astral body will grow finer and the colours more beautiful. The permanence of the aura depends upon the steady maintenance of spiritual aspirations and of gentle and refined tastes.

The aura changes very rapidly. The

colours flash up clear and bright sometimes and at other times fade and become dull. Thus the aura may be described as blue at one time and as red or yellow or any other colour at another, and you become confused. The colours of the astral aura change and vary until the soul becomes steadied, and knowing what it wants, introduces into the aura a permanent and constant vibration of devotion or love or spiritual aspiration. Then lasting auric colours are seen, even in the higher auras. That is, the higher mental and celestial will absorb from the lower. The celestial body is the permanent body in the heavens, the 'temple' spoken of in Ancient Mystery schools. In Masonic schools the building of the temple symbolises the building of the celestial body.

The extent of the aura will vary. That of an undeveloped person will appear to a depth of five, six, seven or even twelve inches. It will seem rather like a fog. When the soul has developed its higher consciousness, the aura becomes steadier and no longer floats and wafts about. Among the masses who know nothing about the spirit life the aura is very indeterminate and may be composed chiefly of murky reds and browns and a strong orange brown. The baser instincts emanating from the desire-elemental are introduced into the aura through the browns and blacks.

The astral body of the ordinary person, as we have said, can range from dull murky colours, misty and indefinite, to a very beautiful, well-formed aura, egg-like in shape, composed of definite and harmonious colours.

Extending again beyond this astral aura can be seen a similar egg-shaped form, but of finer, more ethereal matter, and this is the aura of the mental body. It also can change rapidly with changing thoughts. Beyond and inter-penetrating this to a fine degree is the aura of the celestial or heavenly body, of beautiful form, and of colours almost impossible to describe, because their earth equivalent is hardly known. To this celestial body or aura the ego of the man finally withdraws after he has passed through the experiences of earth, of the astral body, including the Summerland, and of the mental life. All these conditions of life can only be contacted through your corresponding auras.

Do not mistake us; the auras of ordinary good, kindly and helpful people will be pleasant to look upon, but not very permanent or strong. The darker colours will be found at the base of the aura and the more beautiful above the solar plexus.

In a highly evolved ego, the aura may extend to several feet, and in the case of an adept or master as far as a mile or more! So, when a kindly, evolved ego comes into our presence, although we cannot see the spirit, most of us can feel or even smell the aura. The aura has a perfume which, with a master or adept, is quite unmistakable. The aura of any highly evolved ego will bring its own harmony with it. If you are in meditation, and a great one draws near, you may hear his coming announced by strains of music. Possibly some of you have experienced this.

We have been asked what exactly is seen when, apparently, the body of an adept is described by a clairvoyant. It may be a thought projection from the adept or it may be a projection of his astral body. In the case of a young pupil becoming aware of a beneficent presence that blesses and leaves its essence in the aura, that is a thought projection. But where there is definite work to be done, and conversation passes, it will be a projection of the astral body.

While on earth you are building your auras, contributing through your desires to the astral body, and through the astral to the mental and celestial bodies. You are building that celestial body by your actions and reactions, your thoughts and desires. You are doing more: you are creating substance out of the higher ethers which will in due time manifest again on the earth plane, when you reincarnate.

So you see, in spite of little grumbles, that it is you yourselves who have created your present physical body.

When living in that higher state, in that celestial condition, from which man descends to reincarnate, he realises that he needs certain material. He is not satisfied with his temple. He knows that the only way to find more and better material is to return again to a life of form and so *earn* it. All material unused in the celestial body drops away and is consumed; only that which is useful is retained. This we may call the permanent or seed atom. This permanent atom provides for the creation of the vehicles we shall inhabit during our next incarnation. You will see how essential it is to respond to the guidance of the spirit and not allow the body-elemental to dominate!

Prayer is a very powerful instrument to be used with due sincerity and humility. Pray for one single thing, and that is God's love; pray for an increase of God's light, not for yourself, but in order that others may benefit and be blessed through that light. That is the best way to pray. Pray for God, pray for good for your brother, and resign all to God. 'Not my way, O God, but Thy way. Into Thy loving keeping I commit all those whom I love; Thy will be done on earth as it is being done in Thy heaven world.'

III

COMMUNICATION
BETWEEN TWO WORLDS

We would help you to raise your consciousness to the spheres where harmony, truth and love prevail. The whole purpose of the unfoldment of these inner powers, which all men possess in greater or lesser degree, is that you may become aware of spirit, and be enabled to receive impressions of harmony and truth from the spirit world and the spirit people.

Truth is a spiritual law, a reality reflecting the law of God. But we have to prepare ourselves physically, mentally and spiritually, before we can reflect the truth which exists in the spirit world.

We have heard much talk about psychic matters and the proofs of an after-life obtainable through psychic evidence, with great emphasis laid on the *scientific* viewpoint, rather suggesting thereby that the spiritual viewpoint is not scientific. This idea we would correct, and make clear that there is nothing unscientific in spiritual law.

Spiritual law is eternally true, while the pronouncements of science change almost yearly, so that what is considered true today will be dismissed and forgotten tomorrow. With spiritual law there is no change other than continual unfoldment and growth. More and more truth becomes revealed to a man as his inner-self grows in awareness, but the law remains constant.

Spiritual science is the true science, both on earth and in the higher worlds. When a man becomes aware of, practises and *lives* these cosmic and spiritual laws he is truly a man of science.

First, then, let us understand that spiritual unfoldment of a man's inner faculties is an altogether scientific process. If you ignore the laws of God, chaos somewhere in your being will be the result. But if you study the laws of God and abide by them, if you obey the inner promptings of your spirit and go steadfastly forward step by step on the path which lies before you, you will discover a deep well of wisdom within your heart; and also cause your aura to expand so that it reaches out to touch both the heights and the depths of life.

Notice that we have said the 'depths.' Man's consciousness and awareness must extend *both ways*, reaching to both ends of the scale. Your consciousness and aura must expand to embrace the height, the depth and the breadth of life, and in the process of this expansion you will acquire great tolerance, great love towards life and your fellow creatures, and a deep calm and tranquillity of spirit. You will no longer be shocked or repelled by anything; you will accept and understand that humanity in all its stages is in process of evolution or return towards God, from Whom all came.

The unfoldment of your inner faculties is the process through which you will acquire inward strength and poise, and this will purify, strengthen and restore your body to health. It is scientific to say that the inflow of divine light through the heart-chakra and circulating through all the bodies, physical, etheric, astral, mental and celestial, beautifies and strengthens all.

A spiritual man or woman is not weak. Do away with the idea that to be spiritual entails being sensitive and shrinking. True, certain psychics are like frail flowers blown hither and thither by any harsh wind, but this is due to an unbalanced sensitivity, which fails to bring health of body or outlook, rather than to spiritual growth. Resolve to tread the safer path of true character building; and by learning to express greater love to your fellows expand the aura in a spiritual, scientific way. If physical science will agree to be directed by spiritual science, as some day it will, then some of the secrets enshrined in the Ancient Wisdom will be restored to mankind.

As the spiritual awareness of mankind grows, the veil between the earth and the astral world will gradually thin, and the close proximity of the two will become more apparent. Experience such as astral travel will become possible, and even common to man while still in the flesh, exemplifying the unreality of death. As you grow in spirit, a certainty stronger than any conviction obtainable by the study of evidence will grow in your heart, until it is part of your very being. The so-called dead have never died! You will know beyond all doubt that your own dead are with you, but your conviction will be based not on proof or evidence of the outer mind, but on an inward awareness from which nothing can shake you.

Astral Planes

When the quickening of the inborn psychic faculties takes place difficulties and confusion may arise, often through a person's lack of experience, for this link with the astral may not reach beyond what we are going to call 'the plane of illusion,' or the plane immediately surrounding the earth. Nevertheless, psychic contact with this realm can teach many valuable, though sometimes painful lessons. One of the most important of these lessons is that of *discrimination*, or the power to sort out the true from the false.

Do not think of the astral planes as being far removed from the earth; in fact they are so close that many schools of occult thought regard astral life more or less as an extension of man's life on earth, differing not in kind but in degree. Thus it will be seen that the influence of those in the astral worlds must extend to those on earth, and that man's own thoughts and feelings must in turn influence and affect the people in the astral world. The inhabitants of the coarser and more degraded astral spheres can reach men of like tastes on earth and thus obtain experience, at secondhand, of sensation once gratified on earth. Many people on the lower astral planes crave to return to physical life to gratify their desires through contact with the earth, but by your wisdom and love they can be helped, and by helping them you can in turn assist and protect those on earth whom they would degrade.

When the soul leaves the physical body at death, in most cases it speedily traverses the nearby astral planes. During its journey all kinds of memories will crowd in upon the soul. This condition is not real, nor should it last long. But if the soul's interest has centred mainly upon material things during its earth life, it will still cling to the illusion of matter after the death of the body, and will therefore take longer to reach the higher worlds of truth and reality.

There will come a stage in your development when you will most surely contact this world of illusion, and it will be a subtle and disturbing but ultimately valuable experience. You may receive messages which will appear to you to be reliable, and yet you will eventually be disillusioned and disappointed. Do not be disheartened by these experiences. They are all in the course of your training, and it is better for you to suffer disappointment than to evade the experience altogether. It is a condition of consciousness through which every soul must pass.

All of you have the ability to receive impressions and true communications from beings in other worlds; all of you are mediums in that you can be receptive to the spirit; but the quality of the message received will depend upon the quality of your own soul consciousness. Through this contact with the world of illusion you will gain the power to recognise truth, to discern the true from the false. The earth life is full of deception, and things and people are not always as they seem. An important part of your spiritual unfoldment is to develop a true sense of discrimination.

Messages which appear untrue are not necessarily mischievous in intention. They may be given to you purposely to help you to gain poise and strength. Do not think of them as evil, but learn to take them wisely and with discretion. If your teacher is giving you messages, he will be concerned first and foremost with the whole plan of spiritual evolution. His love for you is pure and beyond personal limitation: his one thought and ideal is not for one individual alone, but for the good of the whole. Messages which flatter you and promise much of a personal or selfish nature may be sent to test you.

In spiritual development apparently conflicting statements or paradoxes can arise. But ponder carefully all that is said. If statements seem contradictory, try to reconcile them. Truth has always more than one aspect and many paths lead to God. Therefore do not be dogmatic; do not condemn anything or any individual, and let your approach to truth be orderly, systematic and patient.

Psychic Communication

We would have you realise that spiritualistic communication was a first and necessary step in the preparation of men's minds and understanding for the reception of higher truth. The spiritualist found by experiment that he was able to contact many conditions and varieties of souls in those places surrounding the earth, and of these not all were helpful, and some were the reverse. But the way to obtain more perfect communication is by striving for selflessness and by the strengthening and perfecting of your character. No shadowed soul from the planes of illusion can obtain entry into your aura unless there is some point of contact, some darkened spot which attracts it; it is then that confusion or mischief is wrought. We say again that no disquieted or distressed soul can enter your aura or hurt you in any way once you resolve with all your being to exclude it, for then the entrance has been sealed and you have become master in your own house. No one can ever hurt you unless some weakness, foolishness or vanity in yourself invites the experience.

It is right in certain circumstances to try to bridge the gulf between the recently discarnate soul and the bereaved. It is as if someone dear to us, gone on a long journey, managed to send back to us messages of assurance, telling of his safe arrival, good health and happiness in his new country. Or there may be some wrong that the newly arrived soul ardently desires to set right; or the bereaved person left behind is seen to be in need of help and comfort.

For these reasons or others equally valid it is right to seek communication through a medium; but communication having once been established, and peace and comfort brought to souls on both sides of the veil, it should be realised that both the bereaved person and the loved one in spirit have essential work waiting for them to do, a life of their own to live and personal responsibilities to shoulder. Do not thrust your cares and responsibilities on the spirit world by asking for direction on matters you should certainly decide upon and handle for yourself. Be courageous, and take up life again with a good heart, for in so doing you will grow ever closer to your loved one in spirit.

Some spirits come back with a special mission to help people on earth. Among these are those guides and helpers who spend long years in establishing communication between the two spheres of existence. Their service is both sacrificial and valuable and it should be treasured, and the hours given to this form of communication regarded as sacred.

Not every one who passes onwards to the next world comes back to communicate with people on earth. Therefore do not feel too much distressed if no tidings come for a period from some particular loved one. Know that they have gone to prepare a place, and that your outer life and theirs (which has now become an *inner* life) must lie apart for a period until you have learned to release your own inner-self so that it may reach out to them.

Our whole aim is to help each one of you to unfold soul qualities, so that a sweet and serene communion between those in the spirit world and yourself becomes not only possible, but natural and right.

In spirit there can be no separation. Only *self* separates, and much of the sting of bereavement is due to self. Be pitiless when you analyse yourself; ascertain how much of your bitter resentment at your loss and subsequent loneliness arises from the promptings of egotism and self-pity. Put these aside when you seek communion, for they may hurt both you and your loved one.

Why do you think or feel separate and alone when all things grow towards unity? Each life is as a drop of water in an ocean, a drop which can unite or remain separate from its ocean, but it is ever water and so part of the whole. So also (to change our analogy) each human spirit is a God in embryo; and humanity as a whole is a concourse of tiny God-cells, all linked with God in at-one-ment. Each retains the power to isolate or separate itself from its fellows, but not from God.

Man's innermost self is of the essence of God. Man is formed in the image of God, in His likeness. When man fully realises this transcendent truth, all that is base and worldly will be dispelled. Then man will no longer think and feel in terms of 'here' and 'there,' but of an *everywhere*, where nothing can ever separate itself from God, where no one lives for self alone, and tears, sorrow and death have lost their hold over man.

Your personal self is both your sheath and bondage, and when all your thoughts and feelings centre round the personal self, the real you is shut in like a prisoner. Beneath the outer self lies the individuality, the true man, from which links and threads of interest, sympathy and love reach out to every other soul, to every living creature, to life seen and unseen, to the angel world, to Christ, to God. This must be so, because no other course is open to the inner self.

It must share itself with all that lives, and its only bond or limitation is the boundary of the universe itself.

We are made in His image; the whole universe is God's; and man also is good, is God.

IV

WISDOM FROM BEYOND THE VEIL

You all desire to be used by the higher influences, by the guides and teachers of the spiritual life; and although some of you may already know about your guide, you may not yet realise how you can be used by the Elder Brethren. You may not understand that your own guide is working under the direction of the Elder Brethren, and that while using you the Elder Brethren are also able to assist you in your spiritual growth.

When you selflessly desire to be used to inspire, to heal, to guide and bless humanity, you are bound to absorb into your aura the beneficent light of the spirit. As a servant of the light the guide will then draw close. And remember that all can be mediums; you may all be used according to your particular gifts. You may be a healer, a teacher, a musician, a writer, an artist: whatever your contribution to humanity, as you strive to attune yourself to the invisible planes so you will be used as a channel or a medium for the wise ones in the world beyond.

Let us remind you that each one of you has come back into incarnation to develop a certain quality, which will be built into your higher body, your temple in the heaven world.

An initiate has built into the higher spiritual body all the qualities necessary to make a God-conscious man, and when this has been achieved there is no reincarnation for the soul, except when of its own desire it comes back to help mankind.

But we must stress that you are all, as yet, very human; certain spiritual qualities are only partially developed, and there is also a certain amount of denser matter interwoven or built into the astral body. When you fail to control passion, or to control your thoughts and emotions you cause a hold up in your spiritual circulation. You are not giving the purest vibrations to your guides and to those Elder Brethren who are waiting to use you. So strive for control—control of the physical body, control of the emotions, control of the mind—not so much by sheer will-power, but by aspiring continually in everyday life to touch the pure and holy planes of life.

Spirit is light. Man's higher spiritual self, called by some people the 'causal' body, is a body of light; and as you aspire to realms of light you absorb through the heart, the head and the throat centres of your subtle bodies these qualities of the illumined life. I wonder if you can understand and interpret this?

The Halls of Learning

Some of you are taken during your sleeping hours to the Halls of Learning in the spirit world, where you listen to the teaching of one of the great Masters of Wisdom and perhaps are trained for some particular work. You receive truths which you store up, so that when you return, provided you keep attuned to the heaven world, new ideas suddenly flash into your mind. At such times you think, 'Oh, a brainwave! How did I come to think of that?' What has really happened is that as your physical mind has grown more receptive to inspiration from your higher mind, you have become aware of some truth you have learnt in the Halls of Wisdom in the heavens. Or perhaps, as you write, a wave of inspiration will come and you begin to wonder, is this only something from my subconscious mind, or is this really a message from my guide? Your guide can use your higher mind to frame truths which your brain must clothe with words before they can be expressed in speech or writing, but the essence of wisdom that the message contains will have come from your guide.

Not all men and women are ready for spiritual contact. They may have to accomplish certain work to mould themselves and their character by more material means, and therefore seem unable to respond to spiritual influences. But you have set your feet upon the path of spiritual unfoldment, and you are being guided, inspired and watched over, both in your inner or soul life and in your outer life in the world. Step by step you are progressing, and opportunities are being offered to you, although you may not recognise them as such, which are to test your faith, your loyalty to your higher self and the spiritual powers which encompass you. If there are difficulties in your material conditions, look upon them as opportunities given to you for the purpose of helping you to develop certain qualities you lack, perhaps patience, perseverance, faith, courage, goodwill.

You can be very sure that not one of you is ever forgotten. No soul which is ready to be used as a channel can ever be overlooked by the higher ones, because the awakened soul is a light and can be seen instantly. Your earth, as we see it, is usually shrouded in mist, although some places are slightly luminous. But men and women on the probationary path of spiritual development stand out like stars on a dark night and are known by their light.

The Nature of Evidence

One of the major stumbling blocks hindering the development of mediumship is the desire for so-called 'evidence.' You set a certain standard for evidence; your guide may perhaps give a message through your mind, and your lower self desires proof, saying, 'Yes, but give me evidence that you are who you claim to be. Cannot you tell me what my grandmother is doing in America?' You know the kind of question that is chosen. It is very unwise. Never ask stupid questions of your guide, because when you doubt and set these foolish tests you put in motion vibrations which penetrate into the lower astral plane, and link up with mischievous spirits who will enjoy having a game with a doubting Thomas.

Remember the words of the wise Master who said, '*By their fruits ye shall know them.*' To this some of you may reply, 'Yes, but St. John said, "*Try the spirits, whether they are of God.*" ' By all means test them, but not according to your standards. Instead examine their message. If it has a ring of truth, humility and love, you will not need to test further. *By their fruits ye shall know them.* May we add that your guide and teacher will never issue commands, because this would be breaking one of the spiritual laws. God has given power of free will choice to all His children, although there is an urge which compels you seemingly against your own desires or choice. When this happens it is your own soul and spirit taking charge. The higher ones never dare to interfere with man's free will. When asked for guidance they will point out the way, even show you possibilities which lie waiting along it, but the final decision must always rest with you.

Your Guide and Teacher

Perhaps you are already consciously in contact with your guide? You recognise his personality, feel his gentle companionship? On the other hand, you may still have doubts; on the outer plane you are not quite sure. But if in humility of spirit you could look into the mirror of truth, you would see that a wise and loving guide waits at your side to help you.

What is the work of your guide? He is your companion and teacher, and he works through your higher mind and conscience. You may, as you sit in meditation, ask him a question mentally, such as the meaning of some happening which puzzles you. You may not receive an immediate answer, but, perhaps when you least expect it, in a few days or even weeks, when your earthly mind is engaged elsewhere, suddenly your answer will come. But you will have to remember not to make unreasonable demands on him. Ask, as you would ask an earthly teacher, the explanation of some problem, and the answer will come, perhaps not in your time, but in the time of the spirit. But do not then demand that your teacher shall do the work for you, or expect that he will shoulder your responsibilities.

It is vitally important for every soul to make its own effort and to aspire. According to his degree of effort man is helped onward and upward by his guide and teacher. It is not good complacently to leave all the work to your guide, which is a mistake many people make. It is man's duty to do the best he can. According to his physical equipment he ought to perfect the gifts which God has given him, using his own effort, but remembering that however perfect he makes his mind and however much knowledge he acquires, he is only an instrument, and until he learns the magical secret of connecting himself with the true source of wisdom, he will remain empty. As soon as he can make this connection he opens himself to the inflow of the Christ-Light, and is able to see and feel the presence of those guiding him from the higher planes.

How are these guides chosen or selected and why do they come? First of all, let us try to distinguish between your guide and other helpers from the spirit world. A helper may be brought by the lords of karma to assist you over a certain stage on your journey. It may be that you have asked for aid; for who has not cried out in anguish, 'Oh God, help me!' God hears your prayer; the lords of karma are ever watchful; your guardian angel is on duty, and there are other souls in the spirit world and on the astral plane who may desire to pay a debt they owe you from the past. Such a soul may say, 'Let me go to his help,' and he will come and work for your good, give you guidance and protection as you are climbing the difficult path. His work completed, he will go back again to his own sphere.

Thus you may have many helpers during your life who come at different times to assist you through some particular period, but only one teacher and guide, who has you in his or her care, and who may be attached to you through a number of lives. This spiritual teacher contacts you at a much higher level than the helpers who are so often described as 'guides.' You receive his or her guidance through your conscience, or the voice of your higher self, sometimes called the voice of God. That still, small voice within can become very strong; it can become for you the voice of your spiritual teacher contacting you on the highest level of your earthly consciousness, or the highest level that you can attain while imprisoned in the flesh. All that is lovely and pure and true will come through from your higher self, and that is the level on which your spiritual teacher works.

Would that we could convey to you a picture of your helpers and your guides. If the veil could be drawn aside you would indeed feel happy and thankful that by the power of God, through the will of God, these spiritual brothers come close to help you on your upward climb. We beg you to believe. Try to feel the comfort of their warm handclasp, their hand upon your shoulder, their understanding. Your own spiritual teacher and guide knows every aspiration and every difficulty that you endure, and that guide loves you more than you can love yourself. He is with you to help you in every possible way. You are comrades, and the guide often smooths your path. You have all had demonstrations of miraculous guidance and help. They may be little things perhaps, but you know that they could not have happened in any other way but by spiritual help. Although the law of karma is exact, just, perfect and true, remember that God is a God of mercy as well as justice, and God has a way, through His ministers of light, of smoothing the rough corners. God's love blesses and helps you.

Your Guardian Angel

Christians were once brought up to believe in the reality of angels, but today angels do not fit in with man's intellectual conception of the universe. They are regarded as mythical beings or figments of the imagination. The very idea has grown so nebulous and remote that you find it difficult to conceive a real and living being who holds your soul in its keeping. But the wise man who knows through his intuition, who listens to and obeys the still, small voice, realises that somewhere in the background is his guardian angel.

We speak truly when we say that every soul on earth is in the care of a guardian angel appointed by the great lords of karma. Even the idea of a recording angel has been forgotten, but we tell you that an angel has been appointed to watch over your actions and your response either to the voice of God, or to the tempting of the Devil, which is another word for the lower mind. These ministering angels have not incarnated upon earth, they have evolved along another life path to reach the angelic kingdom. Do not therefore confuse these angelic beings with your guide and helpers. Although your guide and helpers can draw close and commune with you and have their place in the great plan of God, their service to humanity is different from the service given by the angels.

Your guardian angel never leaves you. From the moment of your entering upon mortal life to the time when you leave it, and even afterwards, your guardian angel is in touch with you. It is concerned with your karma and directs your life under the control of the lords of karma. The angel is impersonal in the sense that its work is to see that you are guided towards opportunities to pay off karmic debts, or opportunities to earn good karma to add to the credit of your account. Thus every experience is an opportunity. Sometimes the lower self may say, 'I don't want to be bothered with this.

Oh, what a nuisance, what a bore! I won't do it!'
And a voice whispers, 'But you ought to do it,
you know!' And the lower self answers, 'Yes, I
know, but I don't want to and I won't!' And
you don't. Such an incident makes a mark
in your ledger.

Do not imagine that all of us are perfect
or that we can all show a clean sheet. But we
point out these things to you so that you may
learn. Don't take them too much to heart,
don't fret too much if you make a blot or two.
And remember there is an invisible power, the
power of love in your hearts, which can erase all
stains.

The man whose heart is filled with love,
is never daunted, is not cast down; he does not
give way to unworthy fears, either about himself,
his physical body, or the welfare of those he loves,
because he has been quickened by the divine
light and power, and therefore nothing can go
wrong. Things only go wrong when the mind
of self starts to fret and rail against the circumstances of life, and you say, 'I am disappointed
because the circumstances of life will not go as
I . . . I . . . I want them to go!' Then suffering and
chaos result, because the contact is cut. If only
you had the strength to live always within the
peace of God, to live in the truth—'Thy will, O

God, be done on earth, in my life. . . . Thy will, not mine!'

But when you *do* fall down and everything seems chaotic, remember that there is a helper by your side. Your guardian angel has seen your fall, but he will not condemn. He does not say, 'I told you so!' Instead, he whispers into your heart, 'Courage . . . I will help you rise again. Look up, look out! God is still in His heaven and all is well.'

Hold fast to this thought, especially at times when blow after blow seems intent on knocking you out. Cultivate a sense of humour, but don't lose the strength in your knees! Get up, and stand firmly on your feet again, remembering that you are being helped willingly and readily by the one at your side. Keep on keeping on and refuse to be downcast. Most of us can be cheerful when everything is going our way, but the strength of the spirit shows when a man can smile when things appear to be all against him. Remember it is through the experiences of this life on earth—and this life alone—that you will learn to reach the higher life. Aspiration towards God and the higher life is what really matters.

Do you know that it is possible for a discarnate spirit to be as closely veiled and shut away from the beauties of the spirit life as one who is encased in a body of flesh? Spiritual work faithfully accomplished here and now will lift the veil and take you into realms of beauty.

V

SPIRITUAL FACULTIES

At the beginning of your creation you lay in the heart of the Logos. All truth lies in that simple and central thought. When you were breathed forth into incarnation, when you departed from the heart of God and found you possessed free will, you used it like a wayward child. As a result you fell into the mire of suffering; there indeed you suffered, and are still suffering. Yet you have never completely severed your contact with the heart of God.

If you would progress to the heart of the mysteries of the Cosmos, your way lies through meditation upon and realisation of the still, small voice, the God within; for all the mysteries of eternity lie within your heart. No book can teach you, although in books mental stimulus can be found. Wisdom comes through the heart. Therefore, 'Be still and know that I am God.'

Yet to know God you must learn to live more abundantly, you must savour life to its fullest, for who can learn more of God who remains isolated from his kind?

It takes a God to know a God; and the man who can witness sordid and even terrible human conditions, who can feel with those who endure such conditions and enter into their suffering, the man who can see in the most depraved person something lovable and human, who can see God in the worst of us, comes close to understanding the mysteries of creation.

So, although it may seem difficult at first, we suggest that you share the joys and sorrows of your fellows, and while maintaining your own poise, cry when they cry, laugh when they laugh, be one with them. You will be amazed at what they have to teach you. Don't shrink from contact with humanity, but try to see the beauty beneath the coarseness and crudity. You must be at-one with human life and never hold yourself aloof from it. *Live* life with your brother man.

You choose your Life

Some people think that few have to endure such troubles as fall to their lot. They feel that if they were in different circumstances they could do so much better. Given a bigger income, for instance, more freedom, more leisure, how much good they could accomplish! They note with sorrow how their neighbour, blessed with the wealth and leisure they envy, seems to ignore or neglect the needs of his fellows.

Beloved children, your life is governed by law, and you find yourselves in exactly the place and with the very circumstances which you yourself have chosen. 'But this is nonsense,' you will say. 'I would never have chosen this life!' This is the outer-self speaking, the mortal mind; but the real self, the divine spirit within, knows the needs of your soul. Think of this God-urge as a radiant light ever guiding your soul on the path. Not a moment of your time need be wasted or misspent. The whole purpose of your life and the purpose behind every human experience is the growth and unfoldment of your soul. If you will delve beneath the surface of experience for wisdom and knowledge, you will hasten this process of growth and unfoldment. It is not what is happening to you on the outer planes; it is neither your circumstances nor the riches which you may or may not possess that matters, but only your inner reaction to those circumstances, your relationship from within to your fellow man and to God. The circumstances of your life are actually a form of initiation through which you are daily passing.

At the present time there is great help being sent to man. Man's spirit is being quickened by an inflow of power and light and love from the beyond. A great impetus sweeps humanity. Some of you have experienced initiation and know that it brings an expansion of consciousness, and gives a vision of the future and a desire to live in such a way as to become attuned to the spirit, so that the soul may more quickly enter the kingdom of heaven.

Yet the average human being remains unconscious of the spirit worlds that interpenetrate his physical life. A heavy curtain obscures the vision of man, so that, unable to register the spiritual, he is only conscious of things which he can contact through his physical senses.

Clairvoyance

Man remains, as it were, imprisoned in the physical body; but there are more subtle and refined states of life within the physical, which may be penetrated. In our seven-fold being—as we have already explained—is the etheric body; which is a duplicate in appearance of the physical body, but it is formed of much finer substance which is invisible to the physical sight. This etheric body merges into or interpenetrates the whole of the physical body. The etheric body consists of two parts, a coarser, and a much finer one, and it operates through the nervous system. At death the whole of the etheric body is withdrawn, and the substance of the coarser part, being very like earth matter, soon disintegrates as the physical body disintegrates.

During the physical life, this etheric body forms the bridge between the soul of man and the finer worlds. Across this bridge and *via* the nervous system and the mental and vital body of the medium, the soul in the spirit world communicates with the earth. The type of message which comes through depends largely upon the character of the medium, the circumstances of his or her life, the condition provided by the medium, and the mental and physical condition of the sitter to whom the message is addressed.

Interpenetrating the dense etheric body is a finer etheric vehicle, which I will call the body of light or vital body, which not only interpenetrates the physical and lower etheric bodies, but also the higher vehicles, the mental, the intuitional and the celestial bodies. There is thus a connecting link between each body, by which spiritual light from the divine can descend through these various bodies until it reaches the coarser etheric, which connects all to the brain and nervous system.

When we talk of ordinary clairvoyance, we refer to that type of vision which is most common. Much misunderstanding exists about the nature of clairvoyance. The denser etheric body in some people may be only loosely attached to the physical body and will very easily slip out. The etheric plane lies so close to the earth that to many spirit people it appears almost as dense and heavy as physical substance itself. The lower etheric registers pictures and reflects them to the earth; some people (whom one might describe as involuntary clairvoyants) can see these forms or pictures as they are reflected on the solar plexus centre. Animals also can sometimes see in this way. In the distant past, before man came into such close contact with dense physical matter, involuntary vision, such as this, was common.

The physical body of the average man is not very receptive to spiritual influences. In the normal man the etheric body slips in with a click, as it were, and is sealed down, the man henceforth being unconscious of its presence.

But, as we have said, there are certain people who have a loose etheric body which can slip out of the physical very easily, and then troubles such as uncontrolled clairvoyance and obsession result. There is a vast difference between this clairvoyance on the lower etheric plane and another type which results from training and correct use of the psychic centres or chakras in the etheric body.

I will describe the difference in this way: stand by the side of a very still lake and see the reflection of the trees and sky in the water. How beautiful is the effect! But if the lake should become ruffled this reflection will be shattered. After all it was only a reflection, a symbol, a play of light and colour. Now direct your vision to the true landscape, the actual trees and the sky, and you will see something which is steady, clear, and to your senses, real. This is the difference between involuntary clairvoyance, which is a registration by the lower etheric body, usually uncontrolled and undeveloped; and the intelligent or trained clairvoyance which receives light or impetus from the plane of divine spirit.

Certain drugs can loosen the etheric body from the physical. An intoxicant will do the same, sending the etheric sometimes to a very unhappy place, as is the case with some unfortunate sufferers from *delirium tremens* when actually their etheric body is registering all the sights and conditions of some low astral plane. An anaesthetic will also drive out the etheric body.

Sometimes its consciousness is active, but it often remains supine and does not convey anything to the memory of the patient on its return.

There is a connection between the etheric body and certain main psychic centres, in the head, at the throat, the heart, the spleen, the solar plexus and the base of the spine. Students of medicine will recognise these centres as focal points of the nervous system. These centres again are connected with different spheres or planes of spiritual life. They are like flowers with petals; as you begin to develop spiritual awareness, these flowerlike centres start to develop; they revolve, they have life and light, and throw out beautiful colours. Your guides and helpers recognise immediately your place on the path by the vibration and light and power they can see in these centres.

Some of you have awakened the psychic centres in a past incarnation, and now that you are reborn these centres throw out light which can loosen the texture of the etheric body and cause what is described as a 'natural' medium or a 'natural' clairvoyant. The true clairvoyant, therefore, is one who has brought back the knowledge how to use these centres of the body intelligently, and can thereby often accomplish great work.

We hope you will not all at once start trying to develop these centres! To do this you need far more knowledge than we are now giving you. The centres begin to radiate when the will and intelligence are directing them towards activity. Usually the centre which first reacts to things outside the physical is that situated at the solar plexus. You say, 'I cannot see or hear, but I *sense*!' If you try to analyse how you 'sense' you do not know. But if you carefully examine what has happened you will discover that the solar plexus has experienced a 'queer' feeling, and so you 'sense' that you feel.

The next is the brow centre, sometimes called the Third Eye, but which we shall term here the 'brow chakra.' This can operate in orderly fashion under the direction of the will and the spiritual self, and will cause the medium to become aware of the spiritual spheres. True clairvoyance is not that vision which suggests that you see something with your physical eye. Clairvoyance lies *within* yourself. You may appear to be looking outward at some object, but actually you are looking deeply into this flowerlike centre or chakra within yourself. Therefore, you may see clairvoyantly with your eyes closed. In fact, you will see better so. You will say, yes, but all that may be only imagination! Imagination is a term too loosely used. Imagination is the door to true spiritual vision.

Do not think that the brow and the solar plexus are the only centres used, for when you touch the intuitional or celestial plane, you will see, not with the brow alone, but with other centres: indeed, the whole being sees. When you reach this plane you register or reflect the spiritual planes *truly*. Through divine love the heart centre begins to pulsate and radiate the most beautiful colours and light and then you become aware of divine truth, and you become a medium or channel of pure truth.

Clairaudience

Every person can, by training, become clairaudient, to a degree at least. Clairaudience is governed by rules similar to those outlined for clairvoyance.

In the newly-born babe hearing is the first sense acquired—hearing, then touch, then sight. Note this, because it has a bearing on spiritual unfoldment. There is an old Hermetic saying: '*As above, so below; as below, so above*'; and experience teaches us the truth of this in both an exoteric and an esoteric sense.

Many think that if they hear what is

known in spiritualistic circles as the direct voice, they are obtaining a clear and unsullied message from their loved ones in the spirit world because no human instrument is used. But this is not so; for the voice heard by the sitter, though not apparently connected with the physical, is in fact produced by the *etheric* throat and vocal organs of the medium. Thus the direct voice, although heard by a physical sense and apparently unconnected with the physical organs of speech, makes demands upon the etheric body of the medium in order to produce sound, and may thus be tinged by the medium's mentality.

In such cases the throat-centre of the medium is used. Now this throat-centre is immediately concerned with clairaudience. You may test this when meditating. Concentrate on your throat-centre and you will find yourself listening; and when you have learnt the power of silence, the quietude of spirit, you will be amazed to discover that your spiritual hearing has become enhanced.

Apart from clairaudience of the etheric type, already touched upon, let us consider spiritual clairaudience, the power to be receptive to sacred sounds or vibrations from the world of pure spirit. All can become receptive to the voice of pure spirit; it speaks in the still, small voice within, the voice of conscience.

Do you not think it strange that although you all long to hear the voice of spirit, probably *the very last thing you want to listen to is the voice of conscience*? With many excuses you silence it; but, beloved children, in listening to that voice lies the true way towards clairaudience, or clear hearing.

The stricter you can be with yourself, the outer self, the outer mind, subduing the personality so that the inner voice or the voice of conscience may be heard, the quicker you may travel the road towards clairaudience.

You should regard yourself as a sounding board able to respond to the vibrations from the higher worlds. The mind can interpret the sound within the silence, which comes to you from the world of pure spirit, and from the higher astral world. The first step is to learn to listen. Do not fear or ignore or silence that inner voice. Admit it; welcome it. Admit it even when it tells you you are wrong. Be thankful you can recognise the voice of conscience, for through it you will develop such a true sounding board that you will hear the angels sing!

Can spiritual things be heard with physical ears? you ask. We say: you will hear within your throat and within your head. It is difficult to convey exactly what we mean, but the voice, the sounds, the harmonies will eventually become more definite even than sounds on the physical plane. It is possible for you, while still in the flesh, to be so raised in consciousness as to hear the melodies of the higher planes clearly, and while in this state to be deaf to noises on the physical plane.

It may interest you to know that thoughts can be actually heard, because they make a vibration at the mental level of life. In the inner world, on all degrees of the astral plane, a thought sent forth will be instantly received by the helper of the particular pupil. A thought from you to your guide will be actually heard.

Spiritual Peace

Do you realise the terrible babble on the etheric plane, so near the physical? Imagine tuning your radio receiver and picking up from the ether about a score of stations at once! Can you imagine the confusion? The thoughts of humanity create noise—noise, not sound. Only on spiritual planes of harmony can we call the vibrations sound, or music. Then imagine passing through that babble, inharmonious, crude and harsh, and reaching upwards towards the planes of spiritual life, each more harmonious and gentle until we reach the very spheres of harmony. On these planes there is music in the atmosphere; the very clothing of the inhabitants vibrates harmony and melody.

Can you appreciate the beauty in some small degree? You may acquire the power to tune in to that divine orchestra. But this is not merely a physical gift, it is a soul gift, it lies within you. You may acquire power to hear more clearly and correctly than is possible on the physical plane. But first there must be harmony, there must be purity, there must be love within.

You are ever enfolded within the spiritual emanation, the spiritual force radiating from the aura of Christ, Who has come forth from the Father-Mother God to protect, to purify and to light the way for all the children of God. You cannot be outside this life of the Son, the Christ. While humanity writhes in agony, while dark souls inflict suffering and ignorant souls suffer, always remember that you are a channel and through you Christ can reach others and lighten their darkness.

This will never be accomplished by preaching alone, but only by the strengthening of your spirit, the growth of the divine mind in you, the radiation from your heart of goodwill and peace; not merely a belief that war is utterly wrong, but a peace which can take you through the day placidly, even joyously, a peace which in the midst of physical conflict remains undisturbed, even as the Master taught through the so-called miracle of stilling the tempest. The Sea of Galilee represents the soul-body storm-tossed by the elements from without. The Master, asleep in the boat, or in the heart of man's being, rises and stills the storm; for is He not the Master, the commander? He *is* peace.

This is what we mean by being peaceful, by living peacefully. You need a continual realisation of your relationship with Christ, with the Father-Mother God. Feel the peace which Christ's angels bring. Do not think of peace as a purely negative condition, for the deeps of peace contain the creative forces of the universe, and the holy words of power sound in the silence. Peace is dynamic even as Love and Wisdom are dynamic: all such spiritual attributes are pregnant with power, a power unattainable without stillness of mind and soul.

Holy Communion

Through the five physical senses the spirit or the divine ego learns to become conscious of the

Father-Mother God; to taste, see, scent, feel and hear the nearness of God. A beautiful ceremony in your church enables people to receive an inner spiritual communion. The partaking of the material bread and wine affects man's higher vehicles for a time; but while there is beauty in the outward form, the letter rather than the spirit of the service can become a prop or convention upon which men rest. Strive to become aware in your church or lodge of the presence of angelic beings, from whom flow certain currents of spiritual force; for these can be absorbed through the heart-centre of any soul striving humbly and simply to realise the spiritual help which the angels can bring. Holy Communion is a raising of the divine in man until that divine momentarily touches the divinity, the glory, the purifying elements which come from the Christ. There is no need for the outward symbols of bread and wine. What is needed is for man to become aware of this outpouring so that his heart can be touched.

These are the true, the real, the eternal things; and the confusion and chaos now reigning upon your earth should be outside your consciousness. The power of the Christ love cannot be overcome. We want you to remember that no enemy can break through the circle of light which you, by your own will and aspiration, can cause to be created around you. The red rose, of which we so often speak, symbolises this gift of divine love to God's children revealed in the Christ, his graciousness, his enduring service to all men; for he will not depart, he will not pass onward into the spheres of light which are prepared for him (and for you also), until every child of God is gathered into His fold. This may seem old-fashioned phraseology, but does it not comfort you to know that all the children of God will some day be caught up in the aura of His love? Then shall earthliness pass away and this dark planet (as it is known in the spheres of light) will have served a splendid purpose in the great plan.

Rest your hearts in love and adoration of the great God, and receive the blessing of the Most High. He is able to do exceeding abundantly.

VI

LIFE IN THE SPIRIT WORLD

The world of spirit is usually associated with the heavenly places, with certain spheres to which man passes on leaving this mortal life. Therefore many people, when told that the spirit world is a state of consciousness within the soul (rather than a place or state somewhere outside this earth), find such teaching very difficult to comprehend. You learn that time and space do not exist in the spirit world, and yet you hear of journeying from place to place, from sphere to sphere. You are told on the one hand that the spirit world is in the planes surrounding the earth, and on the other that the spirit world is within you. How are we to connect the two ideas?

Let us consider the inner consciousness. If you close your eyes and turn your thoughts inward, in time you will find within your soul a life which is very real. You will begin to become aware of a plane of consciousness within, and find that you can alter it by your aspirations. As your thoughts become more beautiful, so the light within appears to grow brighter. If your thoughts remain ugly and dull, the world within remains drab. So we find that the world of spirit is reflected within the mirror of our own soul.

I will give you another illustration. Some people take a country walk and notice very little. They stay unaware of the beauties of nature because they do not reflect or respond to their surroundings. Another soul walking that way will delight in a thousand little details of interest in the hedgerows and fields, in the bird life, in the play of the sunlight and the shadows. He is not merely observant with his physical eye, but is beginning to see with the spiritual eye also. Imagine a third man taking the same walk. He has become more sensitive still to the spiritual life behind the physical form and his field of vision has greatly increased. He will not only see all the physical beauty and charm, but also become aware of the pulsation or vibration of a life which permeates the physical manifestation. His soul will reflect the spirit world.

A similar thing occurs when a man passes from the physical body. If he has been engrossed in material things he will remain in that state when he passes onwards and enters the dense astral world, a world very little different from the physical. Although he may dwell in delightful surroundings the beauty means nothing to him. But the next man is more observant and quicker to appreciate, so he will enter a finer state of life; and the third, who is spiritually quickened, who is aware, will find himself in a glorious spirit world.

With each succeeding incarnation the soul follows this process of growth. When man sheds the coarsest envelope, the physical body, and enters into the next stage, the astral body, unless his soul light has grown bright through earth experience and the development of character, he is unable to see or enter into the beauties of the spirit world. But in the course of the soul's journey it eventually sheds that envelope of astral matter; that which is gross and dense falls away—a process which continues through all grades of astral and mental life, until at last the pure soul enters the heaven world.

Again, unless a man develops strength of character and greatness of soul during his earthly experience, his vision and his environment, even in the heaven world, will be limited. On earth success largely depends upon mental equipment and knowledge, but in the beyond it is all a matter of the richness of life's experience and soul knowledge, of sensitivity to the finer vibrations. This awareness is acquired only through the greatness and humility of the spirit; it does not depend on circumstances, material conditions, or intellect, but on the quality of consciousness, on the man's love, tolerance and sympathy; in other words his greatness of heart and beauty of character.

And now a word about the actual *place* of the spirit world. You will say, 'But if it occupies a place, then it must be somewhere outside our earth, and yet you have just said all is contained within!'

Now astral matter, which is closest to you on earth, interpenetrates physical matter. If a spirit enters your home he does not see the actual walls or furniture, but their astral or etheric counterpart. Because he does not manifest in the third dimension, to him physical matter is simply not there, but astral matter exists and it is that which he sees. It is the same with some beautiful scene; it is the astral counterpart of which the spirit is aware.

Everything physical has this astral counterpart. To the spirit there is a lightness, a translucency in all it sees. Your spirit friends may have their home so close to yours that there may be an actual merging of the two. There is no such thing as space, but only the interpenetration of all spheres of spirit life. All is a question of vibration; and your vision of these things depends on your ability to quicken your vibration so that it is in harmony with the vibration of the astral or spirit world. You do not need to die to enter the inner worlds.

People often ask, 'What do the people in the next life eat? Can they really eat? What do they do there?' Well, there are perfect and delicious fruits in the astral world which the dweller in that world can pluck, or he can have any food he likes; but in higher spheres desire for food fades. Nevertheless, we want you to understand that the spirit world is solid and real, and those who live there can enjoy a banquet—if they want to. They can eat very delicious food and drink a liquid which is equivalent to wine, but is actually a spiritual substance. But all food and fruits are spiritual in essence over there, because they are on a spiritual plane of life. They are, however, just as real to us as your coarse foods are to you. The dwellers in higher spheres can also clothe themselves as they wish in most beautiful soft materials, such as do not exist on earth. We are trying to tell you that life in the spirit world is as real as your earth life, only infinitely more beautiful.

Another question asked sometimes is, 'Do

you grow old in the spirit world? Why is it some-times that we see a spirit man or woman who appears to be old?' There is no age in the astral world, only, shall I say, a time of maturity. A person may appear mature, but never decrepit, always full of life, health and well-being. A spirit can clothe itself as it wishes, and will often visit the earth wearing the appearance of the body it wore at the end of its last incarnation. It will appear like that in order to be recognised, but on return to the astral plane it is again at the perfection of manhood or womanhood. You like to have a change of dress? We too have a ward-robe containing different dresses that we can adopt at will. For instance, we may clothe our-selves as an Easterner, with the typical white robe and turban. We may clothe ourselves as an Atlantean, with a crown of feathers like the 'plumed serpent.' We may be seen sometimes as an American Indian with a crown of eagle's feathers; or we may at will adopt the dress of our incarnation as an Egyptian priest. You also will do the same. Whatever you have been, whatever incarnation you have had, you always have the right to adopt that dress. It is yours. You have grown into it and the clothing belongs to you.

The buildings in the world of spirit are beautiful. There are great laboratories for the use of the scientists, and very wonderful observatories for the astronomers; beautiful art galleries and music rooms; halls for the music lovers, and gardens of exquisite beauty for the gardeners. Every conceivable aspiration and need is supplied in the world beyond this. Beyond and beyond and beyond, there is no limitation to the life of the spirit.

Do not think of life and death as being separate. Do not think of 'here' and 'there,' but endeavour to concentrate upon eternal life. We mean by this try to realise that life is eternally now. Remember that when your companion lays down the body, he or she goes into a life which is an inward, a soul and spiritual state, losing the sense of the crushing burden, the heaviness, the weariness of mortality. On the earth many have to work hard merely to earn the necessities of daily life. They cannot always do their best because of economic pressure, which of course is wrong. When they pass to the world of spirit they are relieved of economic pressure, and employed in work which is their joy. Try to imagine what it is like to work free from all limitation, all fear; to work for the very love of the work. This is how people are employed after death. They work with all time before them. There is no sense of rush or hurry. Their work is a form of soul-expression. They are working because they love what they are doing. They have found rest, they have found peace, they have found love.

The Essence of Life is Spirit

Perhaps a certain sadness comes to you with the passing of youth, but age, as you know it, has no reality. We would have you readjust your outlook and think no longer of the years as adding to your cares, as bringing grey hairs, or liability to sickness and disease, because this is false. Resolutely put aside fears and discourage-ment; delve deep into your own being and find therein a power, not of the earth and not of your body, a power and life which does not know age or sickness, sorrow or fear, but only an eternal hope. You must encourage the growth and expression of this life-spirit within.

The purpose of your creation is unfold-ment, growth; the essence of your life is spirit. Spirit will tell you, if you will allow it to speak, that as surely as the sun rises, eternal life is yours. You need no evidence from us who have passed through the glorious awakening. If you are true to yourself, a voice above the clamour and materiality of the world will say, *I live,*

I am eternal: there is no death!

Adjust your life from this moment so that the spirit within shall rise supreme over all doubt and fear. Many people have received what is called evidence, through a medium, and so are assured of a life beyond death. This is insufficient: it is not enough to be told by a returning soul that life goes on after death. This truth must be experienced. Truth dwells within; it does not come from outward things. When your spirit grows strong within your heart, it will continually, second by second, hour by hour, day by day, remind you that life ever unfolds, ever grows more abundant.

You will reply, 'We have heard this many times, but the mind of man demands proof.' The mind of man will receive the proof for which it clamours, when the real self, the spirit within, asserts itself, for it is stronger than the mind. Then you will be released from the prison of the material mind and be able consciously, through daily experience, to know the life of spirit. Spirit ages not; spirit knows neither grey hair nor weariness; spirit is eternal life.

Something indefinable radiates from some people, a beauty, a truth, a sincerity; they are essentially ageless. In these people you are seeing the light, the spirit, grown to such strength as to overpower the limitations of the years. When such souls pass from the earth plane to the spirit world, they find that life becomes serene, harmonious. There is work to be accomplished but no sense of time, for time is not in the spirit world! We do not separate the earth-plane from the next state of life; we see a close relationship between the two, and in the life of spirit opportunities are offered to every soul, and every soul has to find its way to heaven. No soul is coerced or forced, it grows by a process of unfoldment as a flower unfolds.

Personal and Divine Love

The foundation of all spiritual growth is love. We all like to love and be loved; it is natural and makes life joyous and comfortable. Many of us, however, do not understand love unless we see it manifesting through a human personality, and this is quite right; for did not the great Master say, 'He that loveth not his brother whom he hath seen, how can he love God whom he hath not seen?'

But sometimes the affection, or the emotion, called love is centred largely upon one person. Is this good? Only in so far as the personality is recognised as a window through which true love shines.

To find the root of love we must reach behind all personality and recognise a quality of life which is universal. When we touch the place of true love there is no separation, there is no question of separating any individual from his brother, because all the children of God become one when we truly love. This is difficult, for you will argue that in human life you must centre love upon individuals; that your best love must be reserved for husband, wife, children, friends, sweethearts, those who are nearest and dearest, and that your love for them is of a different quality from that which you feel for others.

You will feel more in harmony, perhaps, more at home, more comfortable with those nearest and dearest to you—that is, for ordinary purposes, for ordinary life, because your nearest and dearest minister to your body and comfort your mind, and separation brings grievous loss; but once you have reached beyond the earthly to the spiritual companionship, to an affinity of spirit, you have touched the whole sphere of love, and you will find and recognise in all humanity that same love which is shown to you through the individual.

In every individual soul there dwells the divine life, that life which you all have in common, and it is that which enables you to feel the emotion of love. Therefore to know the meaning of love we must all seek to find that divine love in all our brethren, and not make the mistake of limiting love to any one individual. This seems a paradox. Through loving the individual you contact divine love, and not in any other way. Until you have mastered this lesson you cannot know what real love is. We see the light shining through individual souls; but in reality we love, not the individual himself, but the quality of love shining through him. No teacher will ever claim personal love. Did not the Master Jesus continually remind his disciples of this truth? 'The words that I speak unto you I speak not of myself: but the Father that dwelleth in me, he doeth the works.' The divine spark in man reveals the Christ to man.

Our Attitude to Life

To come again to practical affairs. How can we make the world a better place? If you will resolve with all your heart and soul and mind that your attitude to mankind, individually and collectively, shall be kind—we ask no more, only that you shall be kind—you will be amazed at the peace you will find.

It seems so simple: 'Be kind.' But take this short message to heart. When the New Year comes you talk about turning over a new leaf, about forming resolutions, but soon these fade away, seeming too difficult to fulfil. As thinking men and women you desire above all things to give service and make good use of your life. Not one is passed over when there is work to be done; and as you resolve this day to be a faithful and true servant of God, so we give you once more the very first step:

Be kind. . . . Be kind to one another.

Analyse this little message and you will be amazed how often we all fall short of being kind. The mind can be arrogant, and the mind says, 'I have a right to reason; and this man, or this woman, is wrong.' When you feel thus, look within and ask, who is wrong? Well, maybe it is I.

If someone injures you, we beg you to change your viewpoint. Whatever the circumstances, however acute the seeming injustice, there can be no injustice in life. You are but working through your karma, reaping what you have sown in the past, or else you are being given an opportunity to learn some valuable lesson. When you can look upon the injury with a thankful heart and be grateful for the lesson you have learned, you take a very big stride upon the path. However difficult you find it to accept our words, in the life-to-come circumstances and conditions will teach you to say, 'My God and my brother, I thank you.'

For this very reason we would have you readjust your attitude towards life and just be kind, kind in your thought, kind in your words, kind in your actions. If you cannot give constructive criticism never criticise at all. Thus your Master taught. Time does not alter the eternal truths, for thus has spoken every great soul, each who stands as a peak of the human race, each Elder Brother who has attained mastership and freedom from bondage.

Beloved, we give you hope. There is nothing to fear in life, except fear. Cast out fear and look forward with hope; not merely a vague hope in your mind, but hope throbbing as a life-force in your heart, a sure hope which tells you that all things work together for good; that God is love and that death does not divide and cannot stay the course of man's progress to the eternal day. If a loved companion or child passes through the veil of death, do not fear separation, for you may go to your beloved now, and he or she can still guide and companion you in your earthly life. Only man's materialism can separate souls who love; death cannot sever them.

So we pray that all may be enkindled by the fires of hope, and press forward determined to grow in spirit, to become more aware of the eternal truths. Thus you may know no more disease or poverty, because as you become in harmony with God and His love, every need of your heart and life will be supplied.

VII

THE MIND IN THE HEART,
AND THE AWOKEN MEMORY
OF REINCARNATION

The place of silence deep within your heart is the source of all truth. Your Master will teach you through the mind within your heart and not through the intellect. You will understand this better if you ponder the words of Jesus: *Whosoever shall not receive the kingdom of God as a little child he shall not enter therein.* To become as a little child means to transfer consciousness from your head-mind to your heart-centre.

Normally you think with your brain; as you read your brain is even now interpreting our words: but many people make the mistake of accepting the intellect as the only reliable judge of truth. The head-centre can indeed play an important part in the spiritual development of man; but do not forget that there is a mind in the heart. The heart is a wonderful organ possessing many more secrets than medical science has yet discovered. It has an etheric counterpart which is important in the growth, life and death of the physical body; it also has a spiritual counterpart which we call the heart-centre or heart-chakra, and in the heart-centre is the jewel, the Christ-Light.

Man has lost so much through Western materialism. He has lost his soul with the development of his mental body. Through too much mental activity the heart-mind or the heart-body is neglected until sorrow or physical pain and suffering intervene. Then the powerful and greedy intellect cannot supply anything which will assuage spiritual pain or comfort the sad and the lonely. Only one thing can support man in his hour of need. This is the light which shines from the mountain top down into man's heart, and carries with it a truth which opens his eyes, so that he learns of the goal of his journey. This brings hope and even joy to the man of sorrow. The little seed, the precious 'jewel within the lotus,' quickens and grows. This is why we continually say that meditation is of the utmost importance if you wish to unfold the true light. Books are all very well; studying comparative religion can be helpful, mental gymnastics can be very exciting, but they cannot give you what this inner light can give. We agree that development of the intellect, *if inspired and guided by the inner light*, will lead to greater powers of comprehension and a quickening of intelligence; but we repeat that it is essential for a soul to strive to develop the mind within the heart, the light within, which is the true light of God, the 'Child of God.' Thus, 'A little child shall lead them' . . . Christ . . . the holy child which resides in the heart.

Do not, therefore, let the head-mind be in command, but seek always to become in tune with the eternal life behind the outward manifestation. Meditate often upon the grandeur and glory of God's universe, so that the heart-mind becomes active. Do not fill the lower mind with trash and trivialities; let it be usefully engaged, and at the same time let your heart meditate upon beautiful, joyous and helpful things. Ask your heart: How best can I serve my brother man? It will reply: By understanding him. Man must realise that he is part of the great universe of God; his heart-centre has to awaken, to radiate affection, to burn as a great fire in the soul. He must learn to live not for himself and his own glorification, but to serve and minister to men, healing the sick, comforting the sorrowful, feeding the hungry. A man's religion must express itself in practical service on earth.

Every man is a universe in himself, and the centre or sun of that universe is the heart, not the head. As the sun is the central point of your solar system, so your heart is the centre of your universe. The spiritual counterpart of the physical sun is the Christ-Light. When the Christ-Light is awakened in the heart, the heart-mind begins to function. The physical sun rules the physical heavens, and the Christ, ruling through the sun or the heart, governs the destiny of every man, and of humanity. Even as the Right Worshipful Master rules in a Masonic Lodge, so the Master in the heart must rule the lodge or temple of man's being. But if the Master is not strong enough to control his lodge, if there are ruffians able to overpower the Master, then chaos, sickness, unhappiness and darkness result. The light fades, and with it joy, happiness, wisdom and beauty.

The Master, the Sun within, must rule the lodge of the human heart, controlling every limb and every organ. Perfect harmony, perfect health will follow. If the heart is cold and dead, then the man has no animation, no warmth of humanity, no radiance. As a man thinks, so will he grow to be.

The Wheel of Rebirth

Within the heart-centre also lies the seed atom deposited by past incarnations, a seed which contains memories of past lives, past failures, past triumphs, even past characteristics which have been welded into the soul. Man's becoming aware of the light or Christ within his heart will restore his understanding and bring back memories of these past lives. Such memories well up in the mind of the heart and can be registered by the brain.

Much confusion exists concerning this great principle or law of reincarnation. Some feel reluctance or repugnance at the very thought of having to reincarnate in a physical body, and cannot understand why, having passed through this physical life and on to the spheres of light, they should be forced to return. There seems to be no reason or logic in this law, and it does not fit in, they say, with their conception of an all-wise and all-loving God.

They think of some beloved friend's passing, his returning from time to time bearing messages and descriptions of the heavenly places in which he lives, and they wonder why, once released, he must be drawn back again to the sorrow of earth life. There seems to be no sense in it. If the soul has absorbed so much of the heavenly light, it seems inconceivable for it to be reborn in lowly or perhaps uncongenial conditions on earth: a transgression of the divine order of love and progress.

Reincarnation is a vast subject and we assure you that the ideas prevailing present but a crude and inadequate description of what really takes place. Until you clearly understand the law of reincarnation most of the deeper problems of life will remain obscure, and you will fail to find justice in life, even though you believe that God is good, all-wise and all-loving. Life is growth, the whole purpose of life on earth is spiritual growth, and there are universal problems which can only be answered by gaining understanding of the process of the soul's evolution. Man, confined by finite mind, has no conception of the true meaning of time. He thinks of three score years and ten, or indeed of a century, as a long period, when in truth it is but a flash. He does not think of incarnation in relation to the whole of life, and because of this he fails to grasp how little can be gleaned from one short period of earth life.

Let us then first consider a human life of three score years and ten; let us consider that one birth, life, and death; then let us compare the life of any ordinary man or woman with the life of godliness expressed by one of the great Teachers or Masters. Take the comparison between the two right home: examine well your own soul.

How many times have you fallen short of your own ideal? It is true that you are human, but you are also divine, and the purpose of life is the full development of divine manhood or the Christ-man: indeed the purpose of creation is that all the sons of God may develop into the fullness and glory of the Christ.

It is sometimes said: 'Oh, so and so is an *old* soul!' But how has that soul *become* wise and strong and radiant? By reason of the discipline of the physical life. Discipline spells growth, and the finest discipline ordained by God, the Father-Mother, is the daily round, the common task.

And yet every soul struggles against it. You will say: 'Yes, we can accept this, but does not the soul have greater opportunities on the astral plane for development?' To a certain degree it does; but remember, the limitations of time and space, the restrictions of physical life, are removed on the next plane; therefore there cannot be discipline of the same nature, and the purpose of reincarnation is discipline. To bear sorrow bravely, to meet success with a humble heart, to share happiness with others can discipline the life.

The true home of the soul is in the celestial realms, a place of beauty and of bliss.

Young souls without earth experience may be likened to babes lying in the womb; they have yet to learn to use their limbs, to kick, to walk and to act. We must remember also that those babes are potential Gods, young creators. God devised physical existence as a means of training the child to use all its faculties.

We can think of no better symbol of man's earthly life than that of the seed planted in the darkness of the earth in order that it may grow into the perfect flower. The perfect flower, the archetypal flower, is created first in the mind of God, and then the seed is planted in the earth to grow to fullness. So is it with you, who are as seeds planted in physical form to grow towards the light until you become perfect sons and daughters of God—the perfect archetypal God-man which God held in His mind in the beginning.

The Greater Self

Conceive first then the soul of man, not as you know it in the personality of everyday life, but as something far greater, which dwells in the heaven world and is an aggregate of all the experience of past incarnations. Personal man represents only a small part of the greater soul which dwells in a higher state of consciousness, although the personality can live in greater or lesser degree in touch with that greater soul, and can draw from it if it will.

In the Mystery Schools of the past this idea was sometimes presented to the neophyte through the symbolism of Masonry. The soul was thought of as a temple in the heavens, and each incarnation as a rough ashlar which, through the experiences of earth life, has its rough places smoothed away, so that it may be placed in the structure of the temple. In the building of the temple there can be no slipshod work; there must be exactness, precision; an irregular block or square will throw the whole building out.

Man has to work upon himself—that self which the ancient Masons described as the 'rough ashlar.' He has to work with hammer and chisel and gavel upon the rough ashlar of his own nature, to turn it into a perfect stone so that it will fit into the temple that God is raising from earth to heaven. Once man understands that he has to work upon himself during his ordinary life, and that not a day passes but that he makes some mark upon his own being, he will then learn to control and master his mind and his emotions.

Man, then, possesses a soul in the heaven world which contains the seed, the spirit, the very essence of God in man which directs the course of life. That is why we say that *God directs the path of life.* That urge which stirs man to the highest, sometimes against the will of the lower mind, or the self-will, is the God within man. And it is this spirit or divine spark which directs the life of the soul, guiding it through many earthly experiences. Each time a part of the soul descends into incarnation it absorbs certain forms of experience necessary for the growth and evolution of the greater soul above. So, according to your growth and development you contribute to that larger self. As you strive on this earth plane in succeeding incarnations you are building that beautiful soul.

We would enlarge your conception of re-incarnation so that you discard the idea of man bobbing backwards and forwards between two worlds. We want you to get a larger, grander idea of the continual growth of God-consciousness taking place within the greater soul which is yours. Sometimes when in deep trouble or distress you may receive a flash of power and light from that self and accomplish or endure something you had previously thought impossible. Or it may be that others known to you have received a like flash, by which the coward has risen to be a hero, the selfish to become selfless. You have no conception of man's potentialities once he can make and hold the contact with that greater self which is his true being.

Never make the mistake, beloved children, of judging any man: never look at a soul and say, 'Poor thing, it is unevolved,' for you do not know what you say. It may be that he who appears degraded is a soul of purity and great beauty in the heaven world. You cannot judge.

Why cannot we remember?

You may ask what proof we can give you of the theory of reincarnation? We answer that spiritual things can only be proved in a spiritual way. Few can give proof of reincarnation (although there are a number of proven instances of it) or indeed any other spiritual truth; but proof will come to you through your own intuition, as a result of your own experience.

The only way that man can attain knowledge of the divine secrets is through the path of love and selflessness. Mind, which has its place in evolution, can never of itself unfold the truth; but it is necessary for the mind to be developed before comprehension can dawn. Man seeks to find truth through much reading, but the heart of truth lies in the spirit, and only you can find truth for yourself: no one else can give it to you. In your search for a clear understanding of re-incarnation you must become acquainted with the man within, your innermost self. When you come face to face with your innermost self you no longer cry for proof: the path of the soul's evolution is known.

You may wonder too why you cannot remember the past; but can you recall the time when you were aged two, three or four? How then can you hope to recall incarnations of hundreds and thousands of years ago? Memory is not in the physical brain, nor can it be found in the astral or the mental bodies with which you have clothed yourself. But when you can function in the higher body, which some call the 'causal' body, and which I will call the temple, your vision will be opened and you will re-member, because you will touch the celestial mind, which is the storehouse of all the past.

How long elapses between each incarna-tion? We cannot lay down any hard and fast rule. We cannot say that man reincarnates every two, three or five hundred years. That would be wrong. If we tell you that man passes out of one body into another immediately we shall be wrong again. If we say that thousands of years elapse between each incarnation we shall still not be giving the whole truth. All depends upon the individual. But it is possible for a soul to re-incarnate quickly for a special purpose.

You will ask: at what stage does the soul enter the body? is it before or at the time of birth? We would say that the soul gradually merges itself into the body as the years advance. At about the age of twenty-one the soul has generally incarnated in full, although we would prefer not to bind ourselves as to time. Contact by the soul with the body of the mother is made before physical conception.

Another question you may ask is, whether it is possible for the soul to retrogress in any one incarnation? We would say that if one misses something beautiful on the road it is advisable to retrace one's steps to find it. Would you call that retrogression? But always remember that it is impossible for one soul to judge another: to judge is to condemn yourself.

You may also ask, do we reincarnate into the same family, and if so, shall we always have the same parents or the same children? No, but members of the same family tend to draw to-gether. The link in fact may sometimes be that of brother or sister, father or son, husband or wife. You are bound by the links of karma both to family and friends, and you tread the evolutionary path together in families and groups. According to your karma you will find love and happiness waiting for you; or perhaps enmity and discord, which it will be your task to change into love.

By his incarnation man is bound to affect that part of the world in which he dwells; such is the law. Man is placed where he may give most nourishment to physical life. He gives and also receives nurture from the earth life.

We do not wish to force the truth of reincarnation upon the reluctant. Nevertheless, reincarnation, like life and death, is a law; whether a man believes it or not makes no difference. It is a little strange that some people seem to think that by saying they do not believe in survival after death, reincarnation or the law of cause and effect, they abolish them.

We stress, however, that man has free will. He is never constrained or coerced, never withdrawn from heaven and cast back to earth willynilly. So long as a man declares, 'I do not want to return,' the answer comes: 'Well, my child, rest awhile; there is no hurry.' God never hurries. It is all a question of the evolution of the individual soul, and when you have reached understanding your one longing will be to get back into harness; your one question, how soon can I go?

We have already suggested that you may tend to think that the soul might learn its lessons and work out its salvation on the astral plane, and that on that plane it will come up against exactly the same kind of conditions as on the earth. But the substance of the astral plane is very different from that of matter. It is more easily moulded by, more malleable to thought. In dark, dense physical matter the soul comes up against a severe lesson, which must be mastered and can only be mastered *in matter*. The whole purpose of creation is spiritual evolution: the soul must master dense matter. It must become wholly master of dense matter because it has within it the God-life, and God is working in matter throughout His own creation. The God within grows and evolves until it has completed its work, which is absolute mastery over its environment. It is easier, much more comfortable, to think of the soul passing away from the bondage of the flesh into another world and working out its salvation in nicer and easier conditions; but it does not happen to work that way.

We would also like to point out that the joy

which comes to a soul who attains mastery over the flesh is incomparable. If we could only convey something of that intense joy of accomplishment gained through physical experience you would then fully understand and rejoice in the opportunities given to the soul to return to earth for fresh adventure.

Many of you have returned to earth because you want to help humanity, not necessarily by going to church and doing good works, but because your very presence in life can be a joy and comfort to those about you; to the family into which you were born, to the family of which you may later become a parent, and to many friends as well. You can serve best, not by scattering your energies and forces, but by *being* a son of God, and by giving warmth and light to help each flower bloom its best in the particular patch of garden in which it is planted.

VIII

KARMA

Through the ages enlightened students of religion have recognised karma as one of the laws governing man's life on earth. All life is governed by law, and if we can once establish firmly in our minds that the law is inescapable it will help us to accept the lessons which face us all. Nevertheless, we would like to readjust the view which presents karma as a kind of punishment visited upon man for his misdeeds.

Man is told that God is love, yet he is compelled to witness the suffering of those he loves, and to suffer himself. He feels indignation, resentment, bitterness at times when he sees a beloved relative or friend undergoing pain which he can do nothing to assuage, or sees his dear one die, seemingly at a time when life holds much promise. He naturally questions the love of God. As he looks across a world torn with bloodshed and suffering, a cry rises from the heart of the man of compassion, 'Where is God, and why does God permit this conflict and suffering?'

Beloved children, pause with us, and think. In every moment of life, God is revealing beauty and love to the heart of man. There is not one of you who has not experienced on occasion a feeling of ecstasy and gratitude indescribable in words. This stirring in the depth of the soul may come while you are on some much enjoyed holiday, or after the passing of a cloud of sorrow. It may be experienced after a reconciliation, or perhaps in the coming of the beloved into your life. Here let us say that this human love is really an answer by God to an inward longing and searching for an ideal, for a companion, for beauty, for God. It is the search for God which urges man to seek his mate; the reaching towards God which is behind all nature.

So God comes and speaks in man's heart, but man not recognising the voice as God's, puts it down to nature. Neverthelesss, all beauty, every emotion of joy and happiness is in very truth an expression of God through the physical organism. We all know the joy to be found in the companionship of a friend who is in harmony with us; and the joy which we find comes from the expression through him (or her), and through our own hearts of something beyond the confines of the human mind.

The mind will never unveil God to man.

God is only found at a certain point on the road of experience. He speaks to man through his heart and when that happens man knows, and he never again questions the love of God. The man who has once become conscious of his Sonship never again questions God's love.

So we come at last to the supreme realisation that God is love and that everything manifesting on earth is an outcome of the love of God.

Divine Mother

Let us pause once again to create for ourselves an ideal of God. Prejudice prevents man today from accepting the idea of the Mother-aspect of God. Yet worship of the divine Motherhood has existed since the beginning of time. All humans once loved a mother. A man's love for his wife, the mother of his children, is an inner voice urging him to see in the mother an expression of divinity.

We would have you meditate sometimes upon the divine Mother, and bow before the ideal of a perfect Mother-love. Turn your thoughts to the Mother-aspect of God, the expression of all that is compassionate, warm, kindly, loving, understanding, remembering that the wise Mother knows what is good for the child, and does not fail in her duty. She will administer correction if need be, but with deep love.

What has all this to do with the outworking of karma? Everything, my brethren. It contains the kernel of the whole truth; for we would reveal karma, or the law of cause and effect, as a law created by divine love, not to punish man but to help him to learn truth. To the child the very word 'lesson' is often repugnant, so we will say that karma presents us with an opportunity to know God. All the experiences of your life come to bring you, in the end, the joy of God.

Thus we see that God is both Mother and Father to man; divine wisdom and divine love, as well as divine power, ever at work behind all forms and in every manifestation of life; so that God's children, sparks of divine love breathed forth from the heart of God, may learn to express that happiness which God knows, and which God has placed as a seed within each soul.

The Purpose of Karma

In the beginning man is as a child, a babe, inno-cent of knowledge of divine law, lacking all experience. A little child must learn to sit, to feed itself, to stand and walk and play, and then by mental development and experience assimilate certain facts about life, and by this process come to manhood. The spirit of man goes through a similar process, commencing with its birth from the Father-Mother God, continuing with its growth in spiritual stature, and culminating with the great return, the reunion or at-one-ment with God.

Without the soul experiencing suffering, physical, mental or spiritual, there would follow no expansion of consciousness, no growth from the unconscious to the self-conscious, and then onwards to the Christ-consciousness. Until a soul itself experiences suffering it remains unconscious of the sufferings of its brother, and thus unable to bind the wounds and administer healing. Pain brings illumination, compassion, understanding. Man learns through pain and suffering as well as through happiness and joy.

In the beginning, the child although innocent, has within itself two aspects which men call good and evil. In its life it will express both, and in this expression of good and evil will accumulate credits and debits on a heavenly balance sheet.

If this truth were once firmly established, if all people could see for themselves that as they sow so will they certainly reap, they would pause before slaying anything that contributes to the beautiful or harmonious in life. Not one of us would willingly slay his brother. The story of Cain and Abel demonstrated this, for when Cain, the aspect of evil, killed Abel and became outcast, he cried out that his sorrow was greater than he could bear. But do you realise that even by an outbreak of violent temper you commit murder? Thoughtless, hasty, cruel words are all murdering something beautiful and good. If you think about this you will realise how much better it is to follow the path of self-discipline and strive always towards God, rather than allow the forces of destruction to crush down the better self. The Son of God within is ever building, ever creating good, but if Cain destroys it he inscribes an item on the liability side of the balance sheet.

We cannot alter our past karma, but we can control that which we make for the future; and therefore, my brethren, accept the wisdom of endeavouring to discipline yourselves to the laws of God. Control yourselves, your thoughts, your speech, be kind and loving. It all boils down to that one thing: be kind and compassionate, and never wilfully inflict pain on any living creature. Those who have learnt how much the thoughtlessness, ignorance, or wilfulness of another can hurt will not be heedless in the future. The Masters of Wisdom never inflict pain; they are all love, all compassion. But they also recognise the law of justice, and know that every life must eventually become balanced and polarised to the Divine Light, the Source of all life.

Every action creates karma, which does not necessarily wait to be discharged in some distant future. Results often face you within a few hours or a few days after the debt has been contracted. Do not think that you can indefinitely put off the day of payment, when you make bad karma; for you know neither the day nor the hour when the Lord will reap. This is simply demonstrated: if you walk along a busy road not looking where you are going, you may fall and be hurt. You say, 'Oh, well, I suppose it is my karma!' Yes, it is your karma, but it is an immediate outworking, and not karma made long ago. Karma teaches us to be careful, precise and God-like in the conduct of our lives. Here we have the whole purpose of karma made plain— that by feeling pain we may gain experience and wisdom.

Suppose a burglar breaks in and robs your house. You may say resignedly, 'Well, it is my karma!' But the point is, has that karma taught you anything? If not, it will return, perhaps in this day of life, perhaps not until several incarnations have passed. The essential thing is that your soul has to learn what it feels like to be robbed, because once you inflicted that very suffering upon another soul. So karma comes to teach us lessons, and while doing so, it is also helping us to understand and help our brother to learn *his* lessons. This raises a subtle point, because the question arises, 'If we are helping our brethren to learn their lessons when we cause them to suffer, does it really much matter?' Well, the law is, do unto others as ye would that they should do unto you; and by hurting your brother you are creating fresh karma which will rebound upon you later, for you will suffer the same pain that you have inflicted. The law works both ways, its one purpose being to awaken the soul to a realisation of the perfect life, the divine life.

The Transmutation of Karma

You will ask, 'Can karma be transmuted by repentance?' To recognise the mistake is half the battle, but there remains the one who has been sinned against. To give service to the soul one has injured will be the natural impulse. If you have hurt someone you are sorry, you are full of compassion: 'Oh, my brother, I am sorry, let me bind your wound.' From that expression of compassion there radiates from you the peace and loveliness and light of God, which warms and comforts.

The question then arises: if bodily suffering and sickness are due to the outworking of karma, is it right to try to help sufferers to overcome such karma by giving spiritual healing?

The story of the good Samaritan illustrates this very point. The good Samaritan always does his best to help or to heal.

What part has the patient to play in such healing? The patient is being offered a magnificent opportunity, which originates from his good karma, to rise above the affliction of body and soul. If the man is wise he will respond to the opportunity and endeavour to learn the lesson which is proffered. In aspiring to God, to Christ, he is raised beyond his karma, and the ill karma is thus worked out or transmuted. Thus the Christ within can raise all men to God.

When you were children you were no doubt taught that the way to salvation was to love Jesus, and that Jesus would save you. You were taught that Jesus gave himself to save the world; that Jesus Christ or the Christ, the Son of God, came down to this earth to save the souls of men. How does He save the souls of men? By creating in them love and the power to love. It is the love of Christ, Christ himself in the human heart, which is the saviour of mankind. That love is symbolised by the rose.

Yet bad karma is created not only by lack of love, but by absence of wisdom, by ignorance. Until a soul experiences for itself, it cannot know or understand or appreciate what love is. Through experience the soul acquires love and wisdom. Thus the white rose stands for the pure and innocent spirit, and the red rose for the spirit or soul of man after it has passed through the depths of human experience and learnt the meaning of love.

When we come to the question of ignorance we get into deep waters. Man is not so ignorant as not to know that selfishness and greed are wrong, yet he persists in them, and in so doing brings suffering upon himself. There is a difference between innocent ignorance and wilful ignorance due to denial of the inner voice.

Behind the practice of Confession and Absolution once lay the idea of cleansing the soul from ignorance and darkness, helping it to arise and seek reunion with God. In cases of sudden conversion the divine inflow so affects the soul that there comes a transmutation, a longing to serve, to give. It is said that Jesus the Christ took upon himself the sins, the karma, of the world; that by His sacrificial life and death He was helping to bear the karma of mankind. In a sense the transmuted soul likewise takes up the karma of his lower brethren but to a lesser degree.

Occasionally an incarnating ego is born into a family where a tendency to certain physical afflictions or diseases exists, because the soul has certain work to accomplish; certain opportunities wait to be presented to it. That soul may or may not, according to its strength, fall a victim to such a disease; it need not succumb; it can so strengthen itself that it does not take that particular way of learning its lesson. We would not accept heredity as a foregone conclusion, because every soul has within it the power to determine to a degree its method of working out its karma. A child may solve its sum in more ways than one, and this is where the factor of man's free will choice operates and can direct his plan of life.

You may ask if karma can be speeded up? Most certainly: more particularly when the soul awakens, for then in the heaven world it is vouchsafed a vision of God in greater or lesser degree, and cries 'I want to reach God; I must get there quickly!' 'Very well, my son,' comes the answer, 'but first you have much to clear away.' So when the time comes for reincarnation the karma is hastened. An incarnation such as this may appear to others sad and painful to a degree, but those who have seen the vision do not mind; they accept the karma, knowing that through it they will reach the goal. Therefore, we cannot judge, we dare not judge another person's life. By our standards what appears an easy life might prove a hard and difficult incarnation for the soul in question; and what appears to others to be a hard life, is lived by the participant with an inward grace, a joy and tranquillity which makes a joy of all experience.

This brings us to the very heart of our teaching. Mankind is often stretched upon a cross in physical life, but as a result of crucifixion the fragrant rose is born within him. This rose, as the mystic knows, stands for the heart of love, for the heart of Christ crucified, for the glory and the wonder of a sacrificial love that blooms for all humanity. You see with horror the sufferings of the world, but you do not look beyond the present. Would you withhold from humanity the sweetness and perfection of the rose?

If God denied suffering to mankind, He would also withhold from man the result of that suffering, that for which you are all striving, for which you are all living, for which you were all created—the indescribable joy of the attainment of Christ-consciousness. You cannot separate the rose from the cross. In the early stages of evolution the rose must gradually bloom upon the cross; and in the advanced stages the cross becomes absorbed into the rose, and the consciousness of Christ in man, man in Christ, is completed. Therefore we would guide you to be dispassionate: do not withhold your sympathy and love, but do not allow your emotions to be misplaced. While you give love and sympathy to the sorrowful, remember that suffering is a way to enlightenment, to the birth of the Christ-consciousness in man. Suffering will pass, will be forgotten, except in the quality of consciousness born within the soul as the result.

You may ask, is it not possible to attain this consciousness by the way of love and happiness? Yes, most truly; but God gave man free will and man chose selfwill. Therefore man chose the way of suffering. But so wise and loving is God that He succours man, blesses man and leads him through suffering to the joy of heaven.

Peace, my brethren, peace be in your hearts, and know that God is good.

IX

HEALING FROM THE SPIRIT

One of the most important aspects of spiritual unfoldment is that of healing. We suggest to all would-be healers that the first necessity is to recognise that they can be channels for the divine life-force, and to learn to think of themselves as sons of God, remembering that they are dependent upon Him for all things.

The healing power will continually flow through you when once you have understood the technique of opening your spiritual senses to the cosmic rays of healing. You can all be instruments of these magnetic and spiritual rays; but some people through ignorance and other causes shut themselves off from this life-force.

Your work as a spiritual healer is to assist, to work in harmony, and if you are permitted, in co-operation with the present known medical system. There are many different types of people on earth; one will respond to a certain form of healing, another to quite a different process. Also it is not wise to spend a long time and much power and work on some physical trouble which could so easily and quickly be put right by material methods or even by surgery. At the same time, the basis of all healing is spiritual, and the day will come when spiritual healing will be recognised and fully established on your earth as a most important service. But man has to evolve spiritually before he can command his body.

Fundamentally, all diseases occur in the body through lack of spiritual light. We might put it another way and say that disease is lack of ease, lack of harmony; and that man is busy during his whole life creating disease, inharmony. Harmony and health are preserved when the life is controlled or directed from the Christ within.

Spiritual healing is strictly scientific. It is the bringing into harmony of the wayward physical atoms. It is the voice of command, which sounds from the heart-centre; and this power operates largely through the healer but also through the patient. Love is the voice of command, bringing the wayward atoms into harmony. They are made to obey the law of divine love. This is the secret of healing. And when the patient, like the healer, becomes *en rapport* with that centre of love he is instantly healed, unconsciously selecting the particular cosmic ray which his soul and body need.

Jesus was the great demonstrator of this divine power. Jesus did not concern himself with the names of the diseases. He always went to the spiritual cause. He healed by pouring the awakening light into the soul. He called, 'Lazarus, come forth!' and Lazarus came forth in his grave clothes. Do you not see the significance of this? Lazarus was shrouded in earthly things; he was as one dead; but the voice of the Master called, 'Lazarus, come forth!' and he rose from the dead. That is the work of the true healer.

You must also remember that there is in the soul an accumulation of karma. In so many instances the cause of illness lies deep within the soul, and it has been built into the astral body from a past life. The astral body is created, as you know, from the actions of the past. Past karma which is built into the astral body manifests sometimes in the form of physical ill, or it may come out in the circumstances of a life. The law of karma is exact; it is just, perfect and true. You cannot interfere with karma, but you can assist your patient to transmute it. If the patient is helped to receive the full inflow of the Christ-Light, he will then help himself; and in that way he will learn by transmutation of his karma instead of by means of the particular disease.

The purpose of karma is to teach. It is to give the individual soul the opportunity to learn lessons, to gain wisdom, to grow in spiritual stature. If the soul is arrogant (which is so often the trouble), if it will not believe, is quite sure that it knows, then there is nothing else for it but to walk the allotted path and endure the physical ill. Yet there are some souls who deliberately choose the way of suffering, but the choice is subconscious.

This brings us to another point: never, never force spiritual healing on others. The soul should come of its own free will to seek spiritual help. The need of the patient is for spiritual light; the purpose of the pain is to lead him towards the light.

This is why, in spiritual healing, we tell you not to be concerned too much with the physical body, and its manifold aches and pains. You are concerned with the soul and with the aura of the patient. It is true that the healer may possess certain magnetic force, or 'animal magnetism,' and give temporary relief to the patient, but that is not enough. In spiritual healing you are healing the soul. In time the body will reflect the soul's health.

True healing takes place on the spiritual plane, and healing power comes from the Divine

Life of the Christ Sphere. According to the purity of the healer, it pours through his subtler vehicles—the mental and vital bodies—and streams forth from his hands and his whole aura. As the mountain stream needs a clear channel, so the healing stream needs a pure aura in the healer. It is not merely the laying on of hands, but the contact with Christ. The essence of Christ can then pour forth and be concentrated or intensified in its action by the healer's mental control. For this reason it will be found that Absent Healing can be as effective as the laying on of hands, if it is properly conducted.

In the invisible rays are certain qualities, certain colours and vibrations, even perfumes, which can be drawn upon by the healer, and then passed through to the patient. Usually when a man falls sick, something is lacking, or there is unbalance in the spiritual being, in the soul of the patient. You, as a healer, are working, in company with the angels, to supply the missing element, to restore balance, health or wholeness to the soul. You are a conductor of these pure spiritual forces, so you yourself must endeavour to be like the priests and priestesses of old. You must attune yourself by pure living, pure thinking, pure action and right behaviour, as a human and spiritual instrument.

Strive with all your heart to maintain yourself in good health. Do not overwork yourself on any plane of life. Follow the rules of pure, healthy living. Live harmoniously within yourself. Live on pure, wholesome fruits of the earth. Breathe in the life of God in full consciousness. Be kind to your body, do not force it to do things which it is unwise for it to do. Do not clog it with smoke. Rest it, cleanse it, feed it with pure food, and attune it to the purer vibrations of the higher ethers. The foundation of all healing is attunement on the healer's part to the forces of nature and of the spirit.

Remember to allow yourselves to be re-charged when you are feeling depleted or tired. One good way to re-charge yourself is to plunge your hands in cold water. Another is to put your hands in mother earth; yet another is to go among trees. Stand with your spine against a stalwart tree and breathe with the tree, breathe in the life-force, and you will be surprised how the life-force will flow into you again. Contact nature when you are feeling depleted and tired; and when you feel really unable to do your work, withdraw. In time, you will learn how to replenish yourself so that you will not get weary.

Relaxation is important for healer and

patient, but relaxation under the control of the higher self. Let the body go absolutely at ease, let the mind relax; and let the celestial body, through the physical, astral and mental bodies, fill the aura with the light of Christ. So few know how to relax, they go about tied up in knots, their faces all screwed up, instead of manifesting relaxation, peace and surrender to the heavenly sphere.

As you strive to become a pure channel for the healing power you will become more sensitive, so we should perhaps tell you how to protect your aura. Immediately you feel a hurtful or negative condition, or think you may be 'picking up something,' protect yourself by folding your aura around you as an angel folds its wings. Do this mentally. It will also help you if you take several deep breaths. Draw in the Great White Light, and clasp your hands over the solar plexus, the right hand placed over the left, and maintain positive thought.

The left hand is the receiving hand and the right is the giving hand. If you hold up your left hand in prayer, asking for the healing power to come to you, it will flow into your left hand. It is like a magnet—all the pulsating life-forces come into it and pass through the body to the right hand and thence to the patient.

The healer's touch should be very gentle; a very gentle and light touch is all that is necessary. The rays extend beyond the finger tips and some way below the palms of the hands. Healers must remember that there is another hand over theirs; their hand is not the instrument, but the conductor.

Never allow yourself to become involved emotionally with a patient. On the earth plane, a medical man may be sympathetic and kind, but if he is wise he will never get involved emotionally with a patient. Emotions must be kept under control in all spiritual work. Ungoverned emotions can break up the finest work and the finest groups. We always teach our children to rise above the weakness of uncontrolled human emotion, for nothing so surely stops a candidate from progressing on the path. The wise man is steady, kind, loving to all, and goes direct to the Great Heart of love and wisdom.

The Power of Thought

Thought can create good health, thought can heal; but thought can also inflict pain and disease, disrupt and destroy the bodily, mental and soul life of man. Science is only on the outermost fringe of comprehension of the power of thought. Thoughts of anger, fear and hate form the root of all suffering and of wars. Thought can also bring forth beauty, harmony, brotherhood, and all else that man longs for. We ourselves work as far as possible with the creative power of thought. We try to avoid all destructive thought. We make it a rule, when giving advice and help, always to be constructive, to see nothing but good; and we do this even though we may be called foolishly optimistic. We know that by seeing only good, by creating good by positive thought, we can help to bring about that which is desirable and good. We do not see or think in terms of pessimism, sadness or death. All is life, all is unfolding, all is ever progressing, all is good, all is God. Therefore would-be healers should work only upon constructive lines.

Never suggest that a patient is likely to die. Admit no such thing as death. See only creation, ever changing, unfolding life. There is no death. Believe that 'while there is life there is hope.' Never anticipate anything but good. It is the work of all true healers to inspire confidence, not doubt or fear; always help the patient to attune himself harmoniously to the perfect law of God. The patient should be helped to develop a clear and holy (or healthy) outlook on life. Right thought is God-thought carried through the whole being. This is a tremendous truth; and if you think about it and meditate on what we are saying, you will grasp what we mean. Right thought is God-thought. It is balanced, loving, pure, holy and kind; it is tolerant and generous. Right thought is a general God-outlook on life.

Spiritual healing is brought about by the power of sincere aspiration. When the thoughts are truly aspiring to the Christ, then the Light of Christ, the rays of Christ are felt in the physical body, and having great power they can reverse the sick order of things. Where darkness is apparent in the physical body, this can be turned into light; and the light takes possession, dominating the body and controlling the physical atoms. This is how miracles are performed, but worldly men and women cannot understand or appreciate this. When we say that thought has the power to do this, we mean of course divine thought, the thought which rises from a pure and aspiring heart. The power which comes when the heart is set upon God can reverse negative to positive, darkness to light.

The Master Jesus said, 'I and my Father are one.' 'The words that I speak unto you, I speak not of myself: but the Father that dwelleth in me, he doeth the works.' Every healer must know the truth of this statement, and every patient must seek to understand this eternal truth; for as soon as you make contact with the Christ Presence, even if it is only for a flash, it is like the sparking or the generating of the power of God within you. You forget earthly limitations and you soar into the higher realms of conscious life, and there you are re-charged with the living God-force. Do not be held by the limitations of the earthly mind.

Do not doubt this power. Clear your conscious mind of all doubt, and know in your heart the truth of these invisible healing rays and the truth of the invisible life.

The Angels of Healing

Very little is known at present on the earth plane about the angels of healing, but as the age advances, many more people will not only feel their presence, they will see them. According to the need, according to the vibration created, so there come to a healing service the angels of different colours clothed in the Light of the Sun. You know that the sunlight is full of the colours of the spectrum; now think of the angels of healing in these beautiful colours. There is nothing dark or ugly. They are all light and purity. These angel beings draw very close to the healer, who contributes the substance which they need to establish contact with those who have sought the healing power. These healing rays can be used to heal not only the physical body of individual man, but also the mind and the dark material conditions which oppress humanity.

The radiation of the pure white magic flowed continually from the heart of Jesus. Any man can still receive in his heart this same radiation from the heart of the Christ; and if his heart keep pure and joyous it can in turn radiate light and healing to all the world.

Spiritual healing is a great work in its spontaneous selflessness. The healer does not think of his own aggrandisement. If he did, he could not heal. He thinks only of the good of others; he thinks only of the alleviation of pain and suffering; of the transmutation of the dense conditions of life into a more heavenly state of being.

So we would say that if you long for spiritual development, for unfoldment of spiritual vision, give yourself in service to heal the sick. The Christ through Jesus of Nazareth said, 'Feed my lambs.' Feed the sick souls of men, through spiritual service, spiritual healing. Thus you will be serving selflessly not only present but future generations; you will be helping God to create a better state of life for all people on earth.

My children, follow the path of service, of true goodness, spontaneous joy in life, and become, in time, like your beloved Master Jesus the Christ—perfect sons of the living God.

SUBJECT INDEX

THE WHITE EAGLE PUBLISHING TRUST

NEW LANDS, LISS, HAMPSHIRE, ENGLAND